Gettin' Some Age on Me

Gettin' Some Age on Me

Social Organization of Older People in a Rural American Community

JOHN VAN WILLIGEN

THE UNIVERSITY PRESS OF KENTUCKY

Publication of this book has been assisted by a grant
from the Gannett Foundation.

Copyright © 1989 by the University Press of Kentucky

Scholarly publisher for the Commonwealth,
serving Bellarmine College, Berea College, Centre
College of Kentucky, Eastern Kentucky University,
The Filson Club, Georgetown College, Kentucky
Historical Society, Kentucky State University,
Morehead State University, Murray State University,
Northern Kentucky University, Transylvania University,
University of Kentucky, University of Louisville,
and Western Kentucky University.

Editorial and Sales Offices: Lexington, Kentucky 40506-0336

Library of Congress Cataloging-in-Publication Data

Van Willigen, John.
    Gettin' some age on me : social organization of older people
in a rural American community / John van Willigen.
        p.   cm.
    Bibliography: p.
    Includes index.
    ISBN 0-8131-1648-1 (alk. paper)
    1. Rural aged—Kentucky.   2. Aged—Kentucky—Social networks.
I. Title.
HQ1064.U6K485 1989
305.2'6'09769—dc19   88-28818

This book is printed on acid-free paper meeting the requirements of the American
National Standard for Permanence of Paper for Printed Library Materials. ⊚

Contents

Tables

Figure

Preface: Growing Old in Rural America

According to the 1980 United States Census there are about 6.5 million older persons living in rural America. The rural subset of the older American population is growing rapidly, first, because the American population as a whole is aging. This trend has been especially apparent in rural settings, where the number of these aged twenty to forty-nine has declined while that of those sixty-five and over has expanded in absolute numbers (Zuiches and Brown 1978). Second, there has been a migration turnaround, which became apparent in the 1980 census (Beale 1975; Beale and Fuguitt 1978; van Willigen, Arcury, and Cromley 1985). Between the 1970 and 1980 censuses the long-term pattern of rural population depletion was reversed. The rural, older segment of the population is now among the most rapidly growing components of the nation's population.

In spite of strong demographic expansion, older rural Americans remain poorly understood, if not mythologized (Coward and Lee 1985:xiii). Only a small portion of the substantial literature about aging deals with rural America (Coward 1979:275). Certainly the situation is improving; researchers are directing more and more attention to understanding the conditions under which aging occurs in rural settings (Krout 1983), and two excellent reviews of the publication on rural aging—*The Elderly in Rural Society* (Coward and Lee 1985) and *The Aged in Rural America* (Krout 1986)—have recently been published. Much of the literature explores aspects of the aging process at the national level, frequently using United States Census or similar large-scale survey data. Demographic processes, for example, are well documented (Aday and Miles 1982; Clifford et al. 1985; Fuguitt and Tordella 1980; Soldo 1980) and very useful for understanding situations in local communities. There is also substantial literature on various areas of policy concern, including economic conditions (Moon 1977; Schultz 1980), health (Lassey and Lassey 1985; Kovar 1977), mental health (Scheidt 1985; Kim and Wilson 1981), social service (Krout 1983; Steinhauer 1981), transportation (Cutler 1975; Cottrell 1971), and housing (Montgomery, Stubbs, and Day 1980; Struyk 1977) at various system levels.

In the introductions to *The Aged in Rural America* (Krout 1986) and *The Elderly in Rural Society* (Coward and Lee 1985) the authors emphasize a fundamentally similar point concerning the life of older people in rural American settings. They contrast idealized images of rural life with the actualities revealed by systematic research. Coward and Lee speak of confronting Americans with a "disheartening set of realities" that are "contrary to popular images of the 'good life' " (1985:3). Krout points out "an idealized view," which he contrasts with the "disadvantaged status of the rural elderly" (1986:7). Their comprehensive and current summaries indicate that the rural old have less income (Auerbach 1976; Coward 1979; Kim 1981), worse housing (Atchley and Miller 1979; Coward 1979; Montgomery, Stubbs, and Day 1980; Weicher 1980), worse health (Lassey, Lassey, and Lee 1980) and less access to health care (Nelson 1980; Rathbone-McCuan 1981) and transportation (Cottrell 1971; Harris 1978; Patton 1975) than those who live in an urban setting. Yet Krout makes the point that the comparative research will not actually allow one to conclude that rural people are worse off than urban (1986:7-8), largely because of wide variation in the methods used to distinguish rural from urban and because of a lack of directly comparative studies. In any case, older people themselves generally give more positive assessments of rural life than urban (Lee and Lassey 1980; Hynson 1976; Donnenwerth, Guy, and Norvell 1978).

An important complement to the studies of narrowly defined policy issues, often at the national level, are what, following Clifford Geertz (1973), could be called the "thick" descriptions of the life of older people in community settings. Such accounts of the aging process are appearing with increasing frequency, but nearly all of them deal with industrial societies and urban settings. Barbara Myerhoff, for example, produced a stunning account of Jewish retirees living in Venice, California, *Number Our Days* (1978), which made exemplary use of participant-observation data, so often part of thick accounts. Also noteworthy is Graham D. Rowles's *Prisoners of Space? Exploring the Geographical Experiences of Older People* (1978), which intimately analyzed the life space of older people in a deteriorating neighborhood of a northeastern industrial city. J. Kevin Eckert's *The Unseen Elderly: A Study of Marginally Subsistent Hotel Dwellers* (1980) presents research on social networks and health in San Diego. Doris Francis's *Will You Still Need Me, Will You Still Feed Me, When I'm 84* provides a rich comparison of the lives of older Jews in Cleveland, Ohio, and Leeds, England (1984), with attention to social network relationships.

At least in part the study reported here is in this genre, for it deals with life in a specific place, uses a wide variety of data, and is, to an extent, in the tradition of interpretive social science. It seeks to understand the social organization of older people in a rural Kentucky county through examination of their social networks. The concept of social organization as used in anthropology sees social behavior as the product of individual choices executed in terms of the existing social structures of a community and the individual's goals and purposes. This perspective, consistent with the cultural ecology, or adaptationist, tradition of anthropological theory guided my research, and I have combined different kinds of analysis to discover how the social relationships of persons of different ages vary. I have also tried to interpret these variations in terms of historical change within the community and through comparison with other communities.

Certainly one of the original motivations for this research was to reexamine some of the basic ideas of mainstream social gerontology in light of social network data. To accomplish this objective I have employed a basic cross-sectional analysis of the structure and quality of the social networks of randomly selected people of different ages. I found that the differences between the networks of people of different ages in this particular community were interpretable in terms of aspects of social gerontology theory. This rather straightforward and somewhat technical examination is placed in a thorough study of past and present community life, whose significance extends far beyond the simple provision of a context for interpretation, as will be apparent in the concluding discussions in Chapter 7. I have also made a controlled comparison with the social networks of older people in other kinds of American communities, using comparable studies. This aspect of my analysis forced a number of conclusions about what is important in shaping social relationships of older Americans, particularly the effects of community and national structures.

What I discovered is that the social involvement of older persons increases until they reach their mid-seventies and then declines. Although the late-life decline is significant, the oldest persons in the study maintain substantial social networks. Results show that the diminution of social involvement is associated with an increase in dependency consistent with an exchange theory of social aging (Dowd 1975; Bengston and Dowd 1980). Comparison with data from the conceptually similar studies clearly indicates that the socioeconomic structure of a community in which a person ages has a much larger effect on social involvement than does age itself. (It is not just a matter of where a person lives, of course, but of how that person came to live there.) Age-related changes within the community are small when compared to variation between communities represented by the studies available for comparison. Moreover, there is a historical pattern of change in the social relationships of older people within the study community toward increased age segregation and decreased social density, revealing a process of convergence with patterns found in American urban communities as represented by the comparison studies.

Because there are apparently no published accounts of network analysis done in aging rural American contexts (although there are studies in preparation), all the comparison studies deal with urban population marginalized to varying extents. It is tempting to attribute differences between these populations and the one I have studied to the effects of rural or urban residence. My research, however, shows that structure, manifested as the political economy, accounts for a substantial component of the social isolation of older people. What is different is not rural versus urban residence but the nature of the operating economic relationships in the community. Structural social isolation will be found in both urban and rural environments.

Some would argue that the changes attributable to structural differences can lower social involvement below the level conceived of as normal. The argument is based on E. Mansell Pattison's somewhat speculative theory that the personal networks of psychologically healthy people tend to have a certain size under optimal conditions. If Pattison is correct, then the differences attributable to structural isolation are crucial, for they can reduce networks to a size below that Pattison identifies as normal (Pattison, Francisco, and Wood 1975).

I have based my analysis on three data sets. The first consists of social network inventories of 139 older people resident in a single rural Kentucky county to which I have given the pseudonym Ridge County. The Kentucky Exchange Network Inventory (KENI), developed to facilitate collection of these inventories, will be discussed in detail later. At this point it is sufficient to note that KENI produces self-reports on the structure and content of an individual's personal network, with special attention to the types and direction of exchange relationships. Each interview produces a schematic of the social world of the person interviewed. The second data set comprises ethnographic information on many aspects of life and culture in Ridge County, both contemporary and historical. This ethnographic data base was used in the development of the Kentucky Exchange Network Inventory to determine relevant categories of exchange. It provides a context of meaning for the interpretation of the more formal network analysis. The third data base consists of the available studies of the social networks of older people in other American communities. The results of these studies figure importantly in the final interpretation of my research. These three factors are intended to reflect and clarify each other, to allow better understanding of the social lives of older people in this particular context.

Although my research focuses on a specific community, the historical processes described are widespread and probably characterize the transformations that have occurred throughout much of American life in the last century. The forces operating at the larger level help to shape local life (Dewalt and Pelto 1985), but the degree of influence varies from community to community. Thus, this account can be generalized to those rural American communities with similar structural features. It may also say something about American communities and their older citizens in general.

Chapter 1 links this study with the relevant literature. I review aspects of social gerontology and social anthropology theory and outline some of the orienting concepts important to my interpretation, indicating some of the motivation for the study as well as providing part of the framework for understanding its outcome. The first chapter concludes with an introduction to a series of parallel studies, which will be reconsidered in a comparative framework in the final chapter. Although these studies are all recent network analyses done with older people in American communities, their value for comparison is problematic because of differences in the way variables are operationalized. In almost all cases examination of the operationalization will show differences in measurement, which represent a significant limit on the development of theory.

The ethnographic data are presented in a number of different ways. Chapter 2 presents a capsule general ethnography, which will be used as a contextual foundation. This starts with a discussion of the material aspects of cultural life, namely the environment, population, and economics, and proceeds to aspects of life such as politics and religion. Ethnographic data are also presented throughout the book to illustrate specific phenomena.

The core of the analysis of the network data is presented in Chapters 4, 5, and 6, each of which examines different aspects of the network data set. These sections are introduced by Chapter 3, which provides some background on the data-collection procedures, with special attention to network analysis. Every chapter but the last is introduced with a short narrative composed from ethnographic observations. These scenes illustrate important principles and characteristic behavior.

The research reported here was supported in part by a grant from the National Institute on Aging and by sabbatical leave provided by the University of Kentucky. A number of people assisted in the research and in producing this book. I thank those people who helped develop the Kentucky Exchange Network Inventory, most especially Carol A. Bryant and Victor Kozlov.

Alvin W. Wolfe, E. Mansell Pattison, and Jay Sokolovsky provided network data-collection instruments and technical information during the planning stages of this research. Information about network data-collection alternatives was provided by H. Russell Bernard. The network data were collected with the assistance of John T. Olive, Carol A. Bryant, Lynn Johnson, Christine Emerson and Lisa Elliot. James S. Boster helped with the analysis of the data, which also benefited from the advice of Edward H. Kifer and training provided by the Inter-university Consortium of Political and Social Research at the University of Michigan. Thomas A. Arcury provided excellent advice on the culture history of rural America as well as assisting with Ridge County data. A number of people contributed to the ethnographic data base; Carol A. Bryant and Jane Bagby were of special help, as was Philip Drucker who died before the completion of the project. Thomas A. Arcury, Albert S. Bacdayan, Billie R. DeWalt, Jon Hendricks, Cynthia Leedham, Sara A. Quandt, Jay Sokolovsky, Jacqueline Van Willigen, and Jeannette L. Van Willigen all made useful critical readings of the manuscript. Gary L. Arndt arranged a summer residence in Summit County, Colorado, where much of the book was written.

I thank the kind people of Ridge County, Kentucky for their assistance, especially Elbert Chandler, Wayne Buckler, Strother Ellis, Jewel Jones, Anna Mae Jones, Donnie King, John King, Jr., Porter Henson, Lillian Linville, Mack Linville, Spurgeon Louderback, Mayme Louderback, Lannis MacConnell, Leila Jean McConnell, Kathryn Marsh, Paul Marsh, Virgil Messer, Lewis Workman, Dee Whitaker, Mary A. Wilson, Bessalee Robinson, Lucian Robinson, Gladys Sweeney, Mabel Stewart, John David Sims, Christine Sims, Bug Woodward, and the people at the courthouse and the senior center. These generous and thoughtful people make Ridge County a good place in which to grow old. The staff of the Cooperative Extension Service of the University of Kentucky in Ridge County was always helpful. I also thank the late Vera Rubin of the Research Institute for the Study of Man for encouragement and support in the development of the original research idea.

I appreciate the support of my wife, Jacqueline; my children, Anne Griffith and Juliana Marie Van Willigen; and my parents, Gilbert and Jeannette L. Van Willigen.

Gettin' Some
Age on Me

1. Age and Social Organization

On Sundays around dinnertime, Aunt Marthy liked to look out her window for people going home after church. For most of her eighty years she had been a member there, although she no longer felt able to attend. The white frame church had stood there across the road since before she could remember.

Most days, she'd sit in the creaky, overstuffed chair placed where she could see both the road that went to the river bridge and her niece's children as they played in her living room. She looked after them most weekdays; Wanda, their recently divorced mother, was working in town. On Sundays the children were gone, although they might come along when their mother stopped by to see how Marthy was and to ask if there was anything she needed from the supermarket in Loganville.

Sundays in early spring were always pleasant. Marthy could feel the warming sun coming in through the front window, making the grass in the front yard green up and the yellow daffodils at the front gate blossom. It was always comforting to see those same green leaves. With warm weather the people at the church always seemed to dress better.

In the distance she heard a few cars start, knowing that some would be driving past her house in a moment. Almost exactly an hour before, the steeple bell had been rung by John Ashcraft telling everyone at Bible school and those waiting out in the parking lot that the preaching service was going to start. She could visualize Brother Wayne preaching from Scripture even though she hadn't been up to church for years. As the hand on her big alarm clock went toward noon, it was as if she could hear him give the invitation for the lost to accept Christ. Most of them at the church knew Aunt Marthy, and many felt a kind of bond with her. Perhaps it was because she was frequently mentioned when the shut-ins were prayed for. Anybody familiar with things called her aunt. It wasn't exactly clear why they called her that. She just seemed to be the kind of person you called aunt; she was old, easy to get along with, without children, and though not exactly poor, she didn't have much. She was from a good family with a reputation for being hardworking and honest. With the people leaving the neatly graveled parking lot, she knew, would be one of the elders, who would stop by to serve her communion, as they had been doing for the last fifteen years.

This Sunday, a little after dinner, an elder, Brother Henry, drove up with a younger man, whom she did not recognize. The two of them sat down on folding chairs near Aunt Marthy's creaky chair with its floral throw and talked. The conversations were always too brief for her, but she understood that they had to visit others. Last Sunday they had talked about gardens, about white half runner green beans and raising tomato seedlings in the tobacco bed. The conversation reminded her that Brother Henry's teen-age son had dropped off a brown paper sack full of tomatoes last August. It bothered her that she could not reciprocate with a few squash or green beans, as she would have in the past. She just couldn't manage a garden anymore; the weeds would take it over. Well, they didn't seem to mind not getting something from her, and she did enjoy the visits.

She could have talked about gardening some more, but abruptly Brother Henry opened his Bible to one of the Gospels and after a comment or two to ease their attention from secular to sacred things read of the Last Supper. Brother Henry filled the clear plastic cup from the container they carried in the small communion service and presented this and a small piece of cracker to her on a tiny stainless steel salver. Brother Henry prayed to bless the cup of grape juice and little piece of broken cracker and to remind her that they represented the blood and body of Christ. They were served to Aunt Marthy as they would be served to all the others they were going to visit that day. They knew that she appreciated the visit. They got up to leave, she thanked them. They talked some more as they slowly inched toward the door and took their leave. This meeting of three people is a routine event in the life of an American community. Along with many other kinds of interactions, it is the concrete substance of social life. This book reports an attempt to understand and interpret the social life of which Aunt Marthy, Brother Henry, and the unnamed younger man are a part. It is concerned with understanding the social life of older people.

Social life must be viewed from three perspectives—individual cognition, community structure, and historical process—which are drawn from both social anthropology and social gerontology. Every person, of whatever age or community, makes choices about social life, but these choices are made in the context of structure, including precedent, constraint, resource availability, incentive, and facilities. Because individual access to choices is limited, it is not possible to speak of an abstract principle of "free choice." Choice includes what people call "cruel choices," such as "choosing" to retire because one has had a stroke, taking an early "retirement" because the plant closes down, or deciding to sell the dairy herd because a new milk-handling regulation would require a large capital investment. For my purposes, choice is culturally constructed, limited and conditioned by individual resources and personality interacting with the structures manifested in a particular community. It is in this special sense that I will use the term in this book. Rather than abandoning the word *choice* altogether, we need to master its subtleties in order to link the structures of the environment to the individual.

The way a person of any age behaves is based on the nature of the community—its role structure, behavioral precedents, political economy, and ideological precedents—as well as the attributes of the individual, including knowledge, resources, position in the political economy, and physical mobility. Although individual cognition provides a useful starting point, analysis needs to be extended further in order to comprehend this complex phenomenon. First, theoretical understanding of the problem of choice and social aging needs to recognize that social behavior is dyadic, and so a theory of social aging should also account for constraints, such as the knowledge and motivations possessed by the persons with whom the individual interacts. Second, individuals vary in their tendency to actively pursue their own ends through their choices. That is, some are more deliberative, if not more calculating, than others. Third, there is a general global cultural dimension that can be added to the mix of ideas associated with choice. This is a society's general toleration of change and deviation as an aspect of the structural context of choice. Robert Redfield spoke of sacred and secular societies in this regard (1941). Fourth, a theory of social aging and behavior should account for the impact of the individual's choice. The effect of choice on the psychological state of the individual has been the dominant research issue in social gerontology, generating a great deal of research on variables such as morale and life satisfaction, but I have not considered it in this study. We should also be aware of the effects of the person's choice on culture. The most striking aspect is that the range of alternatives is structured by the process itself. As Jürgen Habermas notes, "praxis always moves within a reality which reason has imagined for itself" (1971). In a somewhat different intellectual context Frederick Barth spoke of social change as being driven by these kinds of decisions (1967). An important aspect of impact is the effect of the choice on the maintenance of society. Classical functionalism is out of fashion; nevertheless, behavioral choice has an effect on the maintenance of social forms.

The concepts of social organization and social structure underlie and encompass the framework considered here. While both social organization and social structure are the focus of extensive discussions of social anthropology it is sufficient to limit our discussion to Raymond Firth's classic treatment of the contrast. Social structure is a cognitive concept comprising the principles upon which the form of social relations is dependent (Firth 1961:28). According to Firth, structure is concerned with "the ordered relations of the parts to the whole" and "the varying orders of complexity" of these relations (1961:30). It is legitimate to think of social structure as a set of rules or a mental template, which individuals know and in terms of which they act, though these are more apt metaphors than demonstrable truths. Our concept of structure is broad enough to include the less abstract notion of the community-"supplied" alternatives for social interaction, including roles and places for interaction. Social organization, which Firth defined as "the systematic ordering of social relations by acts of choice and decision," provides a useful bridge between structure and social behavior. Social structure sets "a precedent and provide[s] a limitation to the range of alternatives" (Firth 1961:40). Social organization is a concrete phenomenon that can be discovered through the observation of social behavior. Social structure is abstract and less directly observable than social organization. It is shaped, as it shapes social life, by the decisions of individuals. Further, these kinds of structures are also influenced by forces outside the cultural context of specific communities.

Both social organization and social structure can be thought of at either the group or individual level. Both are significant to the study of the social organization of older people. In this book I focus upon social organization at the level of individual social networks. This study is an examination of adaptation, of the outcome of individual processes of "potential adjustment to existing and changing conditions," as John W. Bennett puts it (1976:18). At a microlevel, adaptation is indistinguishable from coping. When the element of time is added the same phenomenon becomes a manifestation of adaptive strategy (Bennett 1969) and even cultural evolution (Campbell 1966). The process of individual adaptation shapes history, which reflects the interplay between individual choice and structure. This dimension comes into play in a variety of settings, of which one of the most apparent is the aging process, as it transforms the meanings of experience. People use their life experiences to evaluate what is going on around them. This is one of the ways in which human beings are bound to time. Moreover, individual choice is one of the factors shaping the available alternatives for social life in a community. Other influences come from beyond the community; these have been studied in the work on the political economy of aging (Estes 1979, 1984, Minkler and Estes 1984).

The concept of political economy is essential to any understanding of social structure. Discussion of the relevance of political economy to social aging has recently intensified (Estes

1979; Minkler and Estes 1984; Estes et al 1984; Dowd 1980; Olson 1982). The conceptualization of political economy I use in this book is consistent with the work of American anthropologist Marvin Harris, who defines political economy as "the organization of reproduction, production, exchange, and consumption within and between bands, villages, chiefdoms, states, and empires" (Harris 1979:53). In a recent publication on the political economy of aging, J. Walton defines it as "the study of the interrelationships between the polity, economy, and society, or more specifically, the reciprocal influences among government . . . the economy, social classes, strata, and status groups. The central problem of the political economy is the manner in which the economy and polity interact in a relationship of reciprocal causation affecting the distribution of social goods" (Walton 1979:9, quoted in Minkler 1984:11). Clearly, political economy is a global concept, which is conceptualized in a variety of ways (Staniland 1985). I see the individual's position in the political economy in terms of the nature of the exchange relationships into which that person enters. The transformations manifested in the political economy of Ridge County through time are seen as changes in how people make a living. The qualities of community life relevant to growing old in this county are to a large extent formed by the interaction of politics and economy in the context of larger regional and national systems. I will consider political economy from the standpoint of the community, but it could also be treated in terms of social class or perhaps a construct such as socioeconomic strata.

One of the defining components of the political economy, according to Marvin Harris, is exchange (1979:53), and indeed, reciprocity in exchange forms an important part of my discussion. It is important to distinguish between generalized and balanced reciprocity (Sahlins 1972). Balanced reciprocity, characteristic of the market segment of an economy, is constituted by a variety of kinds of exchange, but the archetype might be buying and selling among strangers. In this type of exchange something is given and that which is returned is specified as to form, amount and timing. Generalized reciprocity, by contrast, is characteristic of the intrahousehold segment of our economy. It also takes many forms, such as sharing out, hospitality and charity. Here something is given, and although a return may clearly be expected, its form and scheduling is characteristically unspecified. Societies vary substantially in the ratio of balanced to generalized reciprocal transactions. Reciprocal relationships bind society together in both communication and comprehension. Simone de Beauvoir maintains that human beings comprehend each other socially through concrete actions, or praxis (1972:216, based on Sartre, *Critique de la Raison Dialectique*). We know each other from what we do rather than from what we think. Further, in reciprocity, she argues, we incorporate each other into our plans and come to know each other. In her discussion of the elementary nature of reciprocity, she echoes Claude Levi-Strauss, who considered "the notion of reciprocity regarded as the most immediate form of integrating the opposition between the self and others" to be one of three universal mental structures that form the basis of social life (1949:84).

Despite the importance of such community structures as political economy, social gerontology has not made much use of them in developing theory. Use of the community as the unit of analysis has been limited, and social gerontologists have seemed unfamiliar with controlled comparison (Eggan 1954) at this system level. Social gerontology does address the nature of social organization and structure, but the treatment is often implicit and ancillary to other issues. Recently some social gerontologists have developed more concern with the social effects of macrostructures and have demonstrated an emerging understanding of aging in relation to the political economy (Estes et al. 1984, Estes 1979, Olson 1982). It would be productive to consider the theories of social gerontology as commentary on the nature of social organization.

It is not appropriate to thoroughly review theories of social gerontology here, but a brief characterization of some named traditions is in order. The development of contemporary theory in social gerontology starts with the emergence of disengagement theory (Cumming et al. 1960). A highly motivating research paradigm, disengagement theory stimulated a large number of refinements, retests, and critiques (Cumming 1964, Maddox 1964, Hochschild 1975, 1976, Rose 1964, Streib 1968, Henry 1965,

Havighurst, Neugarten, and Tobin 1968); in fact, all of contemporary social gerontological theory is derived from disengagement theory as either refinement, extension, or reaction. This theory defines engagement in terms of the interpenetration of the person and society. A fully engaged person participates in a large number of different roles made available in society. Further, the engaged person feels, according to Elaine Cumming, "an obligation to meet expectations of his role partners" (1964:3-4). In their analysis, Cumming and W.E. Henry (1961) present both psychological and social-structural variables. Disengagement theory is a multifaceted explanation of the reduction and change in social activity that is reported to be characteristic of people as they become older. Disengagement is viewed as a process of mutual withdrawal, which maintains both the social system and the personal gratification of the participants. It is primarily expressed in the decreased social interaction of the aging person, who may withdraw from various types of relations differentially. The process is seen as inevitable and universal, functioning to provide room for new participants. It is on the grounds of universality and inevitability that the theory has drawn the greatest criticism.

Disengagement theory is ultimately concerned with the relationship between behavior and psychological outcomes. The concept itself labels a behavioral tendency, but much of the subsequent research has reflected concern with such concepts as morale or quality of life. Engagement is different from social activity. A disengaged person may remain active in a small number of roles, although probably it is not possible to be "firmly engaged and inactive" (Cumming 1964:6), for to be engaged is to participate in the social structure of a community in a complex way. Cumming and Henry describe disengagement in social structural terms as a "thinning out of the number of members in the social structure surrounding the individual, a diminishing of interaction with these members, and a restructuring of the goals of the system" (1961:37).

An alternative to disengagement theory is activity theory (Maddox 1963, 1968, Blau 1973, Havighurst 1963, Phillips 1957, Gubrium 1973), which seems to exist as an "implicit" theory without formal expression (Rowles 1978:29; Cumming and Henry 1961:13). This conception takes the research of social gerontology even farther from questions of social organization than does disengagement theory. Bruce W. Lemon, Vern L. Bengston, and James A. Peterson define activity as "any regularized or patterned action or pursuit which is regarded as beyond routine physical or personal maintenance." The focal idea in activity theory, they say, is that "there is a positive relationship between activity and life satisfaction, that the greater the role loss, the lower the life satisfaction" (1972:511). The basic tenet of activity theory serves social service programmers well, in that it can be used as a justification of programmed activities for older people. It resonates with L.D. Cain's notion of "ameliorative gerontology" (1959). Yet the research done to test the presence of a positive relationship between activity and such measures of satisfaction as morale and quality of life has produced ambiguous results.

Exchange theory, as developed in social gerontology, was posed as an alternative to the disengagement and activity theories. Among its premises is the view that choice in social interaction is based on a generalized and imperfect cost-benefit rationality expressed through a norm of reciprocity (Gouldner 1960) and that imbalance in an exchange relationship is an expression of power differentials and may be related to withdrawal from interaction (Blau 1947).

Exchange theory makes gingerly use of the idea that people maximize their social relationships. As Vern Bengston and James J. Dowd express it, "Interaction among social actors (either groups or individuals) is sustained over time not, as the functionalists would have it, because there exist normative expectations specifying the maintenance of such an interaction or because such a pattern of interaction fulfills some socially required need; rather, interaction is maintained because individuals find such interaction rewarding—for whatever reasons" (Bengston and Dowd 1980:66). An individual's calculations are influenced, of course, by codes of conduct and other limiters (an example familiar to Americans is the idea of fair play). The principle of reciprocity, or equal value in exchange, is an important component of the theory, and its emphasis on choice fits well with the concept of social organization. From an exchange perspective the decrease in social interaction that characterizes social aging is seen as a manifestation of decreasing power resources (Bengston and Dowd 1980:66-68) to which the indi-

vidual adapts through choice. More than anything exchange
theory explains why people decide to disengage. Thus, it is at
base an extension of disengagement theory that posits a mechanism to explain the utility of disengagement in cognitive terms
and so overcomes a major weakness of disengagement theory,
the lack of basis in human choice. At least part of the "mutual
withdrawal" that is an essential part of the theory requires
choice, and choice involves cognition. Adaptive choice is inconsistent with the oft-criticized notion of "inevitability" that is part
of the original formulation.

In summary, at the general level social gerontology offers a
number of theories relating to age and society, which share a
very strong commitment to understanding the psychological impact of various aspects of social behavior on individuals as they
age. There is relatively little emphasis on the study of the aging
process in terms of social organization, for social gerontology
is less social than psychological. As Mary Wylie notes, "Social
gerontology is fully preoccupied with psychological or socio-
psychological variables at the expense of examining macrolevel
structural factors which might impinge on the aging process"
(1980:238). This emphasis on the psychological adjustment of
each person has tended to "decontextualize" the individual
(Marshall 1986:12).

It seems to me that the usefulness of social gerontology theories is limited by the tendency to categorize them into schools.
Defining them in this way seems to create a situation in which
theories are evaluated on the basis of their weakest components,
a bug-focused approach, which curtails development of a systematic theoretical perspective while it encourages the proliferation of nominally different theories. The naming process
creates a kind of symbolic shorthand that allows polarization of
different explanations, even though they are not necessarily mu-
tually exclusive.

Moreover, much of this theory is bound to a psychological,
ameliorative, and monocultural perspective, although these
problems are being aggressively dealt with in contemporary
work. The ameliorative perspective traps thinking in the framework of a relatively narrow social service viewpoint, promoting
activity theory, for example, as a justification of social service
programs. The enormous psychological bias prevents a recog-

nition that other kinds of work need to be accomplished. My impression is that there is not enough understanding about how people actually behave socially. If units of analysis are made more complex, social gerontology can be productively focused on social relations. Further, in spite of dramatic increases in cross-cultural studies of aging (Bengston 1979; Cowgill and Holmes 1972; Fry et al. 1980, Keith 1982), social gerontology still appears bound to the cultural framework from which it developed. There is virtually no controlled comparison literature, even though Leo W. Simmons showed how productive this approach can be when dealing with tribal people (1945). The biases of social gerontology appear congruent with the interests of what Carroll Estes called the aging enterprise (1984) and its attendant structural interests (Alford 1976). Estes persuasively argues that the research results serve to shape the social reality of older people (Estes 1979: 6-15, Estes and Freeman 1976:539).

Finally, the focus of social gerontology theory on psychology decontextualizes the individual. People exist in time and space, but social gerontology, although concerned with life history, almost entirely ignores community history. Such studies as Carole Haber's *Beyond Sixty-Five, The Dilemma of Old Age in America's Past* (1983) and David Fisher's *Growing Old in America* (1977) show the utility of historical perspectives. Demographers bring interesting historical dimensions to social gerontology.

These limitations seem to call for some changes in focus, which are beginning to be seen in social gerontological research. First, there must be an improved grasp of the relationship between the individual and society in historical context. Victor Marshall (1986) recognizes this need in a discussion of emerging theory in social gerontology, quoting C. Wright Mills's classic, *The Sociological Imagination* (1959:3): "Neither the life of an individual nor the history of a society can be understood without understanding both." Second, there needs to be increased emphasis on descriptive and naturalistic accounts of behavior. What people do and how they themselves explain their actions must be the focus of research. There is insufficient understanding of the shape of people's behavior as people's behavior, not as an array of individuals decomposed into variables (Marshall 1986:12). Social gerontology would also benefit from more standardization of concepts and the use of concepts from social organization studies rather than psychologically oriented proxies. Third, there needs to be more research on individual decision making, what people consider when they make decisions about their social life. Many studies deal with the outcomes of individual choice, but few discuss the actual mechanisms of decision making. Anthropological research on agricultural decision making might provide models (Barlett 1980). Fourth, research should attend to the alternatives for social behavior available in a particular community, taking into account such dimensions as community social structure, ethnic and "racial" patterns (i.e. racism), individual resources, community resources, and the like. These dimensions, though perhaps not consciously recognized, will be manifested in the person's cognition. This research should include a spatial component, perhaps following leads established by Graham Rowles (1978). Fifth, social gerontology research needs to explore the effects of choices on society. The process of social change can be thought of as the outcome of allocation decisions (Barth 1967).

In this book I am concerned with the relationship between age and social organization as well as the characteristics of social organizations as changing institutions in a synchronic and diachronic comparative framework. I have chosen to focus upon the social network, but the social structure of a community is expressed in many other ways that could be used for the kind of analysis presented here. Among the alternatives are the social structures based on coresidence, such as the household, those based on association, such as clubs; and those based on marriage and descent, such as family and kin. While all of these have utility, network has the advantage of being the most general, and it can be defined in comprehensive terms. In addition, a person's network can be operationalized to incorporate all these other dimensions, and the concept can more easily be carried from one cultural context to another than the units based on coresidence, association, or consanguinity and affinity.

In a sense, my research is not about social networks but about the effects on society of political economic structures. Because the facet of society being examined is social network, much of the technical language of this monograph is from the network literature. Social network can be conceptualized in a variety of ways and has been used in a variety of research settings, though its use in the context of aging studies is still relatively rare. J. Clyde Mitchell (1969:27) notes that "we know very little empirical information on the way in which the latent network changes over time, particularly through the life cycle of the individual." Marjorie Lowenthal and Betsy Robinson agree, declaring "We need to learn more about the structural, normative, and the latent characteristics of such networks particularly in regard to age-grading" (1976:450). There is increasing interest in using the network concept in social gerontological research. As Jay Sokolovsky points out, "The growing interest in maintaining elderly segments of our population in the community as well as humanely dealing with their problems has greatly stimulated research interest in social networks that can serve as 'natural systems of support' " (Sokolovsky 1985:1). Later in this chapter I will discuss some of the accumulated research that uses the network concept to better understand the aging process.

The network literature is replete with conceptualizations, the development of which is similar to the development of the role concept. Both role and network concepts deal with the individual in the context of social structure and are the products of cooperation between a number of disciplines. The development of both theories followed a similar trajectory; that is, there was rapid development at the conceptual level but slower development of the capacity to measure the phenomenon. Further, both concepts seem best suited to produce midlevel theory. Special terminology proliferates in network studies. Elizabeth Bott (1971:248-330), J.A. Barnes (1972), J. Clyde Mitchell (1969:1-50), and Jay Sokolovsky (1985), all provide thorough discussions of the network concepts that were used as a foundation for the planning of this research.

Social network can be conceptualized in many ways. It is important to recognize that the network concept reflects a natural part of social life rather than an artificial construct. Although collecting network data is not easy, the operationalizations available are quite naturalistic, and therefore they can be used in a variety of situations or "structural contexts." Thus, network measurement is more direct than measurement of such related similar concepts as social space or the various scales of social interaction.

In an inchoate form network has "always" been part of social science. Certainly it is implied in the idea of social structure. As J.A. Barnes notes, "The presence of social networks has been hailed as a necessary ingredient in any cohesive society" (1972:1). The concept first appeared in the anthropological literature as a metaphor. Barnes quotes A.R. Radcliffe-Brown's article on the social life of native Australians. "Direct observation," writes Radcliffe-Brown, "does reveal to us that these human beings are connected by a complex network of social relations. I use the term 'social structure' to denote this network of social relations" (1940:2). Another example of this use of the term appears in Meyer Fortes's study of kinship of the Tallensi (1949).

Network first appears as an analytical concept with operational definitions, specific measurement strategies, and the discussion of specific properties of social life in the mid-1950s in J.A. Barnes's study of the social relations of Norwegian fishermen. Barnes's use of network analysis in this rural village arose from his dissatisfaction with customary social anthropology analysis techniques. He found, simply, that without consideration of network, social analysis was incomplete. "The image I have," he wrote, "is of a set of points, some of which are joined by lines. The points of the image are people, or sometimes groups, and the lines indicate which people interact with each other. We can, of course, think of the whole of social life as generating a network of this kind" (Barnes 1954, quoted in Mitchell 1969:8). Elizabeth Bott plays an equally important role in the formation of network analysis in her classic study of the social relations of married couples in London (1971, orig. 1964), which served to place network analysis in the urban research context where it flourished. Bott demonstrated the use of a number of network structural variables.

To this day network analysis is employed in urban settings for the simple reason that the techniques of analysis used by social anthropologists in smaller-scale (i.e., rural) communities tended to be overwhelmed in complex urban settings. Networks, neighborhoods, voluntary associations, and other units of analysis smaller than the community became more important in social anthropology as the amount of urban research increased. These and other concepts limited the field of inquiry to more manageable proportions, while they led to better total understanding of social life. Alvin W. Wolfe suggested that network analysis may play the same crucial role in the analysis of complex social settings as kinship analysis did in the study of tribal society (1970:227). The substance of all social networks is persons and their relations with others. It is legitimate to think of these elements in terms of points in a structure and lines of interrelationship. Often, in fact, graphic representations of networks rely on points and lines. Points represent elements in a network and the lines represent relationship, without which there can be no network. At minimum a network consists of two points and a relationship, which could be represented graphically as O——O. The process of characterizing the structural elements and the relationship is, in a sense, the basis of network analysis.

There are at least two general orientations to the study of networks: ego-centered approaches and total-network approaches. Ego-centered approaches focus on a network anchored and referenced to a specific individual, usually termed ego, who is interconnected with others, usually termed alters. Total network approaches focus not on any particular person but on the entire web of interrelations in a social entity, such as a community or other social unit. Per Hage and Frank Harary have provided a systematic and clarifying discussion of total-network concepts in *Structural Models in Anthropology* (1983). The unit of analysis of the egocentric approaches is usually termed the personal network (Mitchell 1969:13), which has been defined as "all or some of the social units (individuals and groups) with whom a particular individual or group is in contact" (Bott 1971:320). Bott has found many equivalents of the term personal network in the literature (1971:320-21), including egocentric network (Mitchell 1969), ambience (Caplow 1955), personal community (Henry, 1958), field (Jay 1964), set (Mayer 1966) and reticulum (Kapferer 1969). The concept of "informal support system" is frequently used as an equivalent of personal network, although this term somewhat expands meaning to include a psychological dimension (Sokolovsky 1985:4). In this framework, informal supports are kin, friends, neighbors, or co-workers and formal supports are human service providers (Sokolovsky 1985:4).

Individual personal networks can be thought of in terms of various orders of complexity. Direct contacts with other individuals are termed first-order contacts. It is also possible to speak of second order relationships—friends of friends, for example—and even tertiary relationships. The pattern of first-order personal relationships—that is, all the persons with whom an individual ego is in contact—is termed the first-order star (Bott 1971:320, Barnes 1972:8). The star is defined without reference to the kinds of relationships that exist between the persons who make up the network. The zone comprises the ego's alters and the relationships between the alters. As Bott writes: "Ego's 'star' consists of the people ego knows, and ego's 'zone' is the same set of people *plus* their interrelationships" (1971:320). It is possible to speak of primary, secondary, and tertiary zones and stars. Although distinctions are usually made between networks, stars, and zones, the term network is usually used to refer to all three.

The orders of relationship are termed actual and potential network linkages (Sokolovsky 1985:5; see also Katz 1966). Potential links are those that can be activated or reached through the direct or actual linkages. The concept of secondary and tertiary zones and stars could be approximated by the concept of personal potential network.

To summarize, the network concept has been used three ways in the literature: as a metaphor referring to the array of social relationships in a society and in two analytical modes. The analytical uses of the term include the total network perspective, which encompasses the total set of interrelations in a social group, and the personal, which references the interrelationships to a single individual. A personal network can be viewed in terms of various orders of relationship. Here, I am concerned with primary stars, an important aspect of the personal network perspective. For the most part I use the term network or personal network for what is technically a first-order, or primary, star. I believe that personal network perspective has more potential for answering questions relevant to the social lives of older people than a total network view. It is conceivable that research could integrate the two. In my research I have concentrated on stars as the unit of analysis partly because of interview costs and because of the lack of an effective technique for collecting zone data from a large number of individuals.

Network analysis can deal with a number of different characteristics of networks. In addition to networks as units, network analysts also consider the characteristics of network links, and in the course of such work they have developed many concepts, some of which were used in this study. J. Clyde Mitchell provides a useful discussion of network characteristics in "The Concept and Use of Social Networks" (1969). Some of the network characteristics he reports have to do with total networks, and these are outside the bounds of my study. More relevant are the concepts applicable to personal networks, especially those I have employed in this research.

Mitchell classifies network characteristics into two broad categories: morphological and interactional. Others speak of network attributes and linkage attributes (Leveton et al, 1979). Morphological characteristics, including density, ranges and reachability, refer to the "relationship or patterning of the links of the network in respect to one another" (1979:12). Interactional characteristics, dealing with the "nature of the links themselves" (1979:12), include content, directedness, durability, intensity, and frequency.

Density, one of the most frequently discussed network concepts, refers "to the extent to which everyone else in a set of ego's contacts knows everyone else" (Mitchell 1969:15). Bott calls a virtually identical conceptualization connectedness (1971:59). In spite of the analytical importance of density, the concept is rarely operationalized because of the practical problems of collecting density data, which I will discuss in the section on data-collection techniques. Density is an especially important variable to measure when the researcher is dealing with norm reinforcement, as did Bott in her study of married couples in London (1971). I have not measured density in Ridge County, but informants repeatedly attested to the generally high density of the community when they said, somewhat hyperbolically, "Here, everybody knows everybody else."

Range is simply the number of persons in direct contact with the person whose network is being analyzed (Kapferer 1969, Mitchell 1969:19). In a more complex conceptualization, this idea

also includes the social heterogeneity of the network alters
(Wheeldon 1969). I employed the range variable in a number of
ways. Clearly it relates well to examination of life-course changes
in social behavior because it is a direct measure. For the most
part, I refer to this variable as network size.

Reachability is an instrumental aspect of network density,
which refers to the extent to which persons in a network can
contact each other, that is, whether ego can use members of his
or her personal network to contact others either within or outside
the first-order personal network (Harary, Norman and Cartwright 1965:32). This dimension, like density, is characterized
by a great deal of conceptualization and relatively little empirical
study. Reachability was not operationalized in this study, although it does present itself in the ethnographic data.

Content is a very frequently used interactional network characteristic, which can be thought of in at least two ways: categorical and interactional. Both approaches are found in the
research literature and in this study, but perhaps categorical
approaches are the more common. In this frame the network
alter is classified in terms of meaningful social categories, such
as friends, neighbors, kin. Certainly other possibilities are also
used. Content can also be operationalized in interactional terms.
That is, it is useful to classify content in terms of the actual
content of the relationship as well as the social identity of the
ego-alter pair. Some examples of interactional content found in
the research literature include political support (Mayer 1966:108),
conversation and gossip (Mitchell 1969:21), and exchange (Kapferer 1969). An important aspect of this variable is complexity.
The contrast between simple and complex relationships is conveyed by the terms uniplex and multiplex. Mitchell (1969:22),
following Max Gluckman (1955:19, 1962:27), defines network
links that "contain only one focus of interaction," as uniplex or
single-stranded and those that "contain more than one content"
as multiplex or multi-stranded. I have also used these categories.
Complexity in network relationship is thought to be related to
"strong" relationships (Kapferer 1969) and the interesting concept "social redundancy" (Frankenberg 1966:278). Redundant
social networks provide the ego with alternatives for seeking aid
or building political coalitions. One problem associated with interpreting complexity as a research variable is that it varies from

community to community. Stable small-scale rural communities tend to have a greater proportion of multiplex relationships in the constituent networks of the community. Directedness is an interactional network variable that can require the description of adjacent networks. Basically directedness refers to whether two individuals nominated each other for inclusion in their networks. Mitchell illustrates the idea, "A person may choose another as his friend without having his choice reciprocated, so that the link between the two is essentially a directed one" (1969:24). In cases where an ego named an alter and the alter did not include the ego within his or her own personal network the relationship would be regarded as directed. If nomination was mutual the relationship would be described as reciprocal. The directedness concept may also be applied in ways other than nomination. Both interaction and exchange relationships may be thought of as either directed or reciprocal. In directed relationships the flow of information or economic goods may be in one direction or another or more or less balanced.

Durability refers to the persistence of a particular network link over time. It is possible to think of durability in at least two temporal frameworks. One is temporary and episodic: the network relationship is activated in episodes, and these episodes have durations. More important is a conception of durability that is more structural, focusing both on the actual interaction and the interaction potential. It is possible to study networks from the standpoint of the stable relationships of a person's personal network as well as those relationships that would be activated in a crisis. Durability is an important measure in the study of age and networks, especially as it is reflected in increases or decreases in range. As Mitchell notes, "It seems possible also that the expansion and contraction of personal networks at different phases of the life-cycle hold out considerable potentialities for understanding the domestic cycle, social maturation and similar problems" (1969:27).

Intensity refers to "the degree to which individuals are prepared to honour obligations, or feel free to exercise the rights implied in their link to some other person" (Mitchell 1969:27). Intensity is thought to be related to a number of other network link qualities. There are those who suggest that relations with kin are likely to have greater intensity than those with neighbors and there are similar propositions about the positive association of multiplexity and intensity. A related concept is strength, which Mitchell defines as "the ability of a person to exert influence over others" (1969:29). Strength and intensity are reciprocals of the same quality of networks. Unfortunately the dimension in either of its incarnations is difficult to measure. Virtually all attempts to measure intensity are based on fieldworker assessment. This strategy probably works well in cases where the research goal is to analyze a limited number of networks, but it is unworkable in research where many standardized measures of many networks are collected.

Frequency, which simply refers to regularity of contact, is somewhat easier to measure than intensity. It is likely that frequency will vary with other network characteristics in different ways in different kinds of economic systems. One would expect, for example, that among industrial laborers many high frequency links would tend to be uniplex. The reverse may be true in family-based agriculture.

In addition to these morphological and interactional network variables it is also useful to speak of the characteristics of the parties to the network, or member attributes (Leveton et al. 1979). Among these features are such variables as sex, age, occupation, residence, ethnicity, and class (Sokolovsky 1985:6).

Clearly, network analysis is rooted in a relatively elaborate set of concepts. As will be apparent when measurement is discussed, however, there is considerable gap between the conceptual development of network analysis and the actual capacity to measure. Many network dimensions are products of reasoning rather than observation.

In addition to recounting the results of my research, I also want to compare my findings with those of similar studies. This comparison will be taken up in the last chapter, but I want to describe the studies I have chosen for comparison here, to provide a basis for interpreting the content of social life in this study. The cases were selected by careful review of recent journal articles and their bibliographies, as well as an on-line search of *Sociological Abstracts*, limited to English sources published in 1975 or later that reported empirical research using social network variables in the context of an older population living in a specified locality. Some studies revealed through this search were rejected for comparison because they did not deal with network as social organization but treated social network as a relatively unspecified variable in a psychological analysis. It is for this reason that no studies of national samples were included in my review. I made no attempt to obtain research reported in dissertations, technical reports, or conference papers. Otherwise, however, I tried to make the search as orderly and comprehensive as possible so my review would be useful for understanding the social networks of older Americans and the status of network studies practice and to provide a framework of comparison for the research reported here.

In "The Cultural Meaning of Personal Networks for the Inner City Elderly" (1978) Jay Sokolovsky and Carl Cohen examined the personal networks of ninety-six elderly residents of ten single-resident-occupancy hotels in midtown Manhattan. Previous studies of this type of living pattern showed a high degree of social isolation. Data were collected on tenants ranging from 60 to 93 years of age, whose mean age was 71.9. The data were collected using what the researchers referred to as the Network Analysis Profile (Sokolovsky and Cohen 1978:328), which was developed for the study. The profile was based on about four months of preliminary fieldwork, including participant observation and some exploratory interviews. The Network Analysis Profile collected data on six "sectors of interaction," that is, relationships with tenants, nontenants, kin, management, public agency or health care professional, and social institution. The inquiry was structured around each of the interaction sectors. In addition, data were collected on characteristics of the alter, expected sites of interaction, modes of transaction, and certain aspects of the emotional nature of the relationship. Each link included data on content of the relationship, frequency, duration, intensity, and directional flow.

Sokolovsky and Cohen found that the mean number of network links was 7.5, with a range of 0 to 26. They also showed that 60 percent of the links were complex multistranded relationships but that about 40 percent reported that their networks did not contain any alters with whom they had intimate relationships. Kin played a relatively minor role in these personal networks. About 70 percent of the networks included kin, but typically only 10 to 20 percent of relationships in a network were with kin. The researchers identified such related network features as structural dispersion, highly selective intimacy and variable activation of ties. By structural dispersion the researchers mean that personal network ties are diversified and that egos "will attempt to avoid getting deeply involved in a single close-knit clustering of friends" (Sokolovsky and Cohen 1978:334). The researchers argue that such dispersion provides for flexibility in their support system. Selective intimacy refers to what the researchers regarded as very limited development of intimate relationships. While they report the development of many complex dyads, these relationships rarely became intimate. The fear and suspicion of the residents seem to have been the most important determinants of the pattern. As the researchers note, "Guiding the perception of the personal world SRO dwellers see around themselves is a good deal of fear and suspicion. They have little control over who will be residing on the other side of their drab wall and often little actual basis for mutuality in social relationships. The vast majority of the limited intimate ties found in their personal networks stem from a long-term association generated through occupational or kinship ties begun in earlier parts of the life cycle" (1978:336). Variable activation of ties refers to the ego's strategic use of the network links to acquire aid, perhaps, for example, maintaining the network link in anticipation of future crisis. One aspect of analysis on which Sokolovsky and Cohen did not report is the relationship between network size and age.

Gloria J. Wentowski reported on "helping behavior" in the personal networks of fifty older people in an urban setting in the southeastern United States in "Reciprocity and the Coping Strategies of Older People: Cultural Dimensions of Network Building" (1981). The research began with "exploratory fieldwork" in settings older people tend to frequent, including neighborhoods, apartment complexes, flea markets, luncheon programs, as well a senior citizens programs. This component of the research process built relationships between the researcher and potential research subjects while it improved the researchers' understanding of how older people "build support over time in their interpersonal relationships" (Wentowski 1981:601). From what was learned during this exploratory phase,

Wentowski developed an interview schedule for collecting network data. Some of the fifty people interviewed were among those met during the preliminary phase of the research, and the others were recruited through their networks. While the sample was non-random, the researcher indicates that she attempted to select subjects with certain regional demographic and economic characteristics. In addition to network variables she collected data on socioeconomic status, health, and various aspects of interests and activity. The network data-collection procedures were less structured and formal than some of the others I am using for comparison. The process involved the composition of a list of network members and the "type and frequency of their activities" (Wentowski 1981:602). At this point the research resembled that typically associated with cognitive anthropology, (see Frake 1962; Spradley 1979; and Tyler 1969). Expressed simply, cognitive anthropologists use a technique referred to as ethnosemantic elicitation to discover how people structure knowledge. Wentowski used such techniques to elicit the research subject's understanding of different helping roles and their content. This approach resulted in, among other things, an analysis of the cognitive domain "kinds of helpers," which impinges only indirectly on the research problems I consider here. More useful are the results concerning network composition and exchange. Wentowski's ethnographic analysis of reciprocity presents a number of useful interpretations of the long-term patterns of exchange.

Another relevant study is "A Reassessment of the Sociability of Long-Term Skid Row Residents: A Social Network Approach" (1981), in which Carl Cohen and Jay Sokolovsky used their Network Analysis Profile instrument to collect data from forty-eight elderly men residing in the Bowery. A general goal of the research was to evaluate the view of skid row residents as socially isolated, which is ubiquitous in the literature on inner city areas like the Bowery of New York City. The version of the Network Analysis Profile they used collected data on "six fields of interaction," including relationships between ego and "hotel contact," "outside nonkin," "kin," "hotel staff," "agency staff," and "social institution" (Cohen and Sokolovsky 1981:97). Only those linkages characterized by a certain minimal frequency level were included, and the measurements of network variables included network size, configuration (a measure based on graphic analysis of density), frequency of interaction, duration of interaction, content (i.e., uniplex and multiplex), and directionality. In addition data were collected on health and psychosocial status.

The skid row study considered only respondents sixty years of age and older. The research subjects were recruited from a lunch program at a senior center, Bowery hotels, and some missions. The mean age of the subjects was 67.1 with a range of 60 to 89. Cohen and Sokolovsky discovered a mean network size of 5.5, with a range of 0 to 21, and they commented, "These aged Bowery men had the smallest networks of any urban population previously studied" (1981:102). The researchers also found that those over seventy years old had smaller networks than the rest of the subjects, but the difference was not significant. Most network alters were fellow hotel dwellers. The frequency of interaction with kin was lower in comparison with other segments of the network, and over half the networks contained no kin at all. About 90 percent of the relationships were multiplex, and except for relations with kin, "reciprocity in relationship was strictly adhered to" (Cohen and Sokolovsky 1981:100).

J. Kevin Eckert has studied the social networks of older people in single-resident-occupancy hotels in a deteriorating area of a major West Coast city, examining the relationship between personal networks and certain health and well-being measures (1980, 1983). Eckert was interested in the effects of forced relocation due to urban renewal on the mental and psychological health of the SRO hotel residents. He used a quasi-experimental design to measure certain variables before and after the move on both relocatees and a similarly situated group of people who were not forced to move. A number of health measures were used, and the network variables were collected using a shortened version of Sokolovsky and Cohen's Network Analysis Profile (1978). Eckert collected data on three "major sectors of interaction"—relatives, immediate environment (i.e., the hotel), and neighborhood—asking each person to list "those persons with whom he or she felt close; the specific nature of the relationship; where the person lived; the frequency of contact in terms of letters, telephone calls, and visiting; and the time at which the contact was last seen" (Eckert 1983:40). The content of the linkages was characterized by means of five categories: giving help during illness, lending or giving money, giving rides, running errands, and discussing problems. The analysis revealed that the social networks of those forced to move were unaffected by relocation. Eckert suggested that because the relocatees were not moved out of the downtown environment their networks were not disrupted. The personal social networks of these SRO residents were characterized by what he termed structural dispersion. That is, the networks had very low density, and when in-hotel ties were lost, neighborhood ties were able to carry the person over the period of dislocation. Such dispersed relationships provided privacy and noninvolvement, whereas the network ties that were spatially closer tended to have their exchange relationships limited to simple errands and nonmaterial exchanges. As Eckert notes, "People try to limit their social debt" (1983:43). Interestingly, kin relationships provided few material exchanges, although they appeared emotionally supportive and had the potential for instrumental exchanges. Another feature of the networks is what Eckert called nodal-based relationships. These are relationships with key individuals within the downtown setting, such as hotel clerks, shopkeepers, waitresses, and bartenders, who are sources for new relationships. After relocation those who had moved simply established relationships with whoever occupied the old roles in the new setting. Eckert, echoing earlier researchers, refers to these persons as the "anonymous service fringe" (1983:44; Boissevain 1974). The networks also manifested what Sokolovsky and Cohen have termed "variable activations of ties" (1978). Eckert focused on an older population (mean age 69.4; range 50-93) but did not attempt to study the effects of age on network composition.

Eckert also found that relocation did not have significant effects on the health of the study population. Persons who rated their health as poor were, however, more susceptible to stress. The social networks of the relocated individuals manifested a capacity to adjust well to change. New relationships were established around existing nodes, the content of relationships changed to compensate for loss, and relatively inactive linkages became more active. In part, the ease with which networks and support were reconstituted after the move related to the fact that most relocatees remained in the downtown area, where they could maintain some network ties to the neighborhood.

The last study I have chosen for comparison was done by Mary Ann Stephens and Murray D. Bernstein, whose research examined what they called "informal helping networks" and "well-being" among residents of two federally aided apartment complexes for old people. These housing facilities required that residents be "ambulatory and independent in activities of daily living" (1984:145). The population had a mean age of 74.6, years with a range of 65 to 88. The network measurement was carried out with the Support Network Inventory, which is designed to "record information on interpersonal relationships deemed important in maintaining one's current style of life" (Stephens and Bernstein 1984:145). The support dimension was measured in a number of ways. Constituents of the helping network were classified as other residents of the apartment complex, relatives, and nonresident friends and associates. In addition, relationships were described in terms of support content, which included casual conversation, entertainment, intimate conversation, advice, transportation, aid with meals, housekeeping, aid with health and finances. Importantly, the direction of the exchange was also noted, as were such other aspects of the network as frequency and value of the relationship. In addition the researcher used a measure of life satisfaction and health status.

The research found that the mean number of helping relationships for the respondents was 5.3, with a range of 2 to 10. Most frequently these relationships were with family members. The size of the helping network was not related to age. Analysis of exchange demonstrated that family and nonresident friends were the most important providers of support. Health was measured in a number of ways. Respondents with sensory impairments had significantly fewer relationships. Those experiencing chronic illnesses had fewer relationships with residents, although their relationships with people outside the complex were the same as those of their healthier coresidents. The life-satisfaction measurement revealed that more satisfied residents had smaller helping networks.

The research showed that exchange relationships in the networks tended to be reciprocal. About one-fourth of the resource exchanges were between residents, and one-fourth were reciprocal. As Stephens and Bernstein note, "the support involved in residents' relationships with other people was not exchanged in one direction but, rather, involved active giving and sharing by these older people" (1984:147).

All these studies share two striking characteristics. First, all focus on urban populations. Second all (with some qualifications about the Wentowski study) deal with residential concentrations of older people. The Wentowski study selected informants from "a variety of settings where older people normally live and re-create neighborhoods, apartment complexes, local flea markets, federally funded luncheons at local churches, and senior citizens' groups and clubs" (1981:601). The fact that my literature search produced no studies of the social networks of rural Americans is consistent with the general pattern of American social gerontology studies. None of these studies are of the older members of the "general population." All involve the selection of a subgroup based on residence or, in the case of the Wentowski study, a combination of residence and activity groups. I could find only one study of older people in the general population, including rural residents. The study, reported by Ronald L. Simons (1984), was based on a comprehensive sampling frame of a "midwestern county," using a mail questionnaire. In this case, the researcher reported that only 2 percent of the respondents were from the countryside. I have omitted this very interesting study from the comparison matrix because it uses social network figuratively, actually examining psychological rather than social organization variables.

The social life of people is a product of individual choice, selecting from the alternative social behaviors in a community. The social alternatives are products of both individual and community histories as well as the political economy. The research I report here must be considered in this complex context. At the most general level the content of my study is defined by the concepts of social organization and structure (Firth 1961) and adaptation (Bennett 1969), all of which turn on individual choice. Social organization deals with the relationship between choice and social structure; adaptation deals with choice and adjustment to circumstances. These concepts, I hope, will allow me to produce a highly contextualized description of the outcome of the processes they imply.

Within this frame my research considered a series of questions related to the social life of older people, addressed from a network perspective. Social network analysis is but one tool that can be employed to better understand social life; it does have some advantages for use with older people. Most important is the elementary nature of such analysis, which provides the potential for more effective comparison. Indeed, it is to facilitate comparison that I have so extensively discussed the alternative ways of measuring and conceptualizing social networks. Many of the more formal questions associated with the network analysis components of this study are consistent with the underlying concern of social gerontology with social life. Casting some of social gerontology's basic concerns with social life-course changes in the framework of social network analysis, however, represents a kind of innovation.

In conjunction with my concern about comparison is my decision to place this research in a framework of recent published accounts of community-based research dealing with older people and employing direct network measures rather than indirect measures. All the research took place in American cities, although this was not a selection criterion. These studies will enable me to include synchronic comparison of different local adaptations.

2. Social Ecology of Ridge County, Kentucky

Luke felt tired and stiff as he leaned over to stoke the sheet-metal stove, glowing a dull red, which stood at the rear of the stripping room. Just last night he had figured out that this was his fifty-second crop of burley tobacco, not counting the two that he missed during the war. Most of the crop had cured out real well. About a quarter of it still hung, brown and lank, in his barn, and Luke planned to take the last of it down Monday night. He was well into the stripping, even though he was having trouble getting help. Like his daddy said, you just had to stick with it. He had decided to bale the last ten rails of tobacco that were still hanging, using his neighbor's baler when he was finished with it. The rest of his market quota of 4,250 pounds was being done the old way, stripped and tied into hands. Most of the really big farmers were baling just about everything, and Luke had already decided that he would switch over, even though the bales looked terrible and the whole idea ran against the grain with him. It was so much easier, what with the trouble hiring extra hands. Nevertheless, a basket of hand-tied tobacco was real pretty.

The wood sputtered and caught fire, and Luke gingerly closed the door of the old stove. He leaned back and took his place next to his younger brother at the stripping bench. Bobby, employed as an assembler at the storm window plant in the next county, had taken a few vacation days to help get the crop stripped out. Luke took off his gloves and dabbed a little Vaseline on his hands, enjoying the slick, clean feel it gave them in spite of the tobacco gum accumulated from the morning's work. As Luke settled back in and took up a stalk from the growing pile that his brother had finished, Bobby spoke, "You're doing pretty good on this stripping. Get any help last week?" Luke answered flatly, concealing his concern about the day-to-day difficulty in getting good help, "Sure. That kid that lives with his mother in the trailer next to the store showed up through Wednesday. Said he never had stripped any tobacco before. Really, he done pretty good. Never did come back Thursday. Could have used him." Bobby sympathized, "Its hard to get good help anymore." Luke, reassuring himself, answered, "Anyway, we've got a right smart of it done."

He was thinking about how many times they had had this little snatch of conversation while they were stripping tobacco or housing it or at any of the other times you needed help. It seemed to him that between the factory work and the welfare, you could not find and could barely afford help. He added a few more leaves to his handful, tied it tight and round, and jammed it onto the tobacco stick protruding from the side of the bench. The conversation drifted over the next two hours, punctuated by laughter now and then about cows getting loose, hay wagons tipping over, and elections being bought. Finally, and predictably, Luke's wife tapped gently on the stripping room door and without coming in said, "Dinner's on."

This chapter is an interpretive ethnography of an area in Kentucky to which I have given the pseudonym Ridge County. This ethnography is intended as a framework through which to understand the social networks of the study population. It will also, I hope, provide a basis for understanding the differences between Ridge County and the locations explored in the network comparison studies. I want, here, to present a kind of social ecology, to demonstrate some of the relationships that exist between society and sectors of culture, both currently and within the lifetime of the oldest members of the community. Ridge County is situated to the north of Lexington, Kentucky, on the edge of the region called the Outer Bluegrass, whose rather steep-sloped terrain differentiates it from the gently rolling land of the Inner Bluegrass, site of the ample Thoroughbred and Standardbred farms with their white or black board fences, vast stables, and mansions. To the east are the mountains, which provide another distinct environment. Ridge Countians see both the bluegrass and the mountain people as different from themselves, both socially and culturally. In a number of ways, it is possible to argue, the county is a bounded social entity.

The first visual impression of Ridge County, whether the observer comes from the bluegrass flatlands or the eastern mountains, is of markedly unusual terrain. Entering from the rolling pasturelands to the south, one passes a small strip of bottomland alongside a river, traverses a short strip of broken step land, emerges onto a rolling alluvial plain, then suddenly zooms up a winding stretch of road onto the crests of a narrow ridge system. The ridge crests are not level but seem relatively so in comparison to the steep hillsides that drop to the "hollers," narrow gullies that bed ephemeral streams a hundred feet or more below the ridge crests. The gullies drain into a few larger permanent streams or creeks, some of which have narrow strips of level bottomland. What is striking is that many of the steep hillsides are mowed hayfield or pastures. Other tracts obviously were also cleared pastures at one time but were subsequently abandoned and are gradually being taken over by stands of eastern red cedar. The major roads follow the crests of the ridges, and most modern housing is perched, often in rows, along the same crests. In addition to the occasional string of modern houses on the main roads, Ridge Countians reside in a single town, some rural villages and in isolated farmsteads. The rural villages are usually arranged in a linear settlement pattern, with perhaps a slight nucleation around a store or a church. In some smaller rural settlements the stores are abandoned.

Anyone familiar with economic life in central Kentucky will grasp the important aspects of the economy simply by driving through on any weekday. Season by season, the work of producing burley tobacco and livestock feed and forage continues. A more informed eye will note the cars of day-migrating factory workers formed up into improvised parking at rural crossroads. Many Ridge Countians raise burley tobacco, some raise cattle; and others work in factories in adjacent counties. Many combine these ways of making a living. A few teach at the school, drive school buses, keep a store, or work at the limited number of other kinds of jobs available within the county. Among those who would describe themselves as retired are farmers who slowly withdrew from farming and, more rarely, those who formerly held wage and salary jobs. Industrial employment is a recent development in Ridge County, where farming used to be primary and where it is still important, still part of most people's thoughts.

Topographically, Ridge County consists of a dendritic ridge system that branches toward the southwest. At the nexus of the ridges is the seat and largest settlement of the county. Off the ridges, ravines, branches, and creeks lead toward the narrow bottoms of the river that marks the southwestern boundary of the county. Although figures are apparently unavailable, one might estimate the amount of level land in the county as about 5 percent of the total. A very small proportion of the county is level bottomland. The steep slopes of the ridges dominate the landscape.

Geologically, the county is formed of four similar rock formations, all part of the shale belt that separates the Inner and Outer Bluegrass regions. All consist of alternating beds of limestones and shales. The soils derived from these formations, either directly or as alluvium, are light, fragile, fertile for agricultural production, and highly subject to erosion. On the plow-damaged hillsides erosion of light topsoils has left heavier soils.

Ridge County soils were probably never as productive as those of the Inner Bluegrass and, under the cultivation techniques of early settlers, suffered more serious erosion because of steep slopes. Nonetheless, agriculture has been the mainstay of the local economy since the beginning of white settlement late in the eighteenth century, and many contemporary Ridge Countians who use modern farming techniques efficiently make a fairly good living from the land.

Best evidence indicates that before white settlement the area was heavily forested. Ridge top and slope soils that developed in place were fairly stable, except under special stresses, such as the shifting of river channels. When early settlers cleared the forests on the ridges and hillsides, rooted out the stumps, plowed and planted the crests and steep slopes, severe erosion began. This effect of European farming techniques was not unique to Ridge County, of course. It occurred throughout the nation, but it was worse on broken terrain like that in Ridge County.

Although no precise measurements are available, many elderly farmers, and younger ones too, refer to the "wearing out" of land by preceding generations, most of whom sold their holdings cheaply or even just abandoned them to move on. A saving grace was that the early farms were small, as was the acreage under cultivation on each farm, because of the use of animal traction until relatively recently. By 1960 the use of animal traction had virtually ceased.

Domestic water is supplied by a municipal water system in the county seat and wells and cisterns "out in the county." Groundwater has always been more easily accessible on the lower- lying alluvium in the southern parts of the county. There, shallow wells can easily be tapped. On the ridge crests, well drilling is likely to be less productive. There is evidence of an aquifer lying beneath the county seat, which may have influenced the siting of the town in an apparently odd location. Generally, the alluvial bottoms have fairly good groundwater systems, but the ridges, comprising 95 percent of Ridge County land, are very sparsely supplied. The less reliable wells of the ridges are often supplemented with cisterns filled with runoff from the roof and with trucked-in water deliveries. A few men supplement their income by hauling water from a public hydrant near the courthouse, driving their sloshing loads on flatbed trucks with tanks attached.

In contrast to the newly constructed homes, early pioneer structures were placed farther down ridge slopes to be nearer water supplies. Today, new construction is mostly perched on the ridge tops and linked to a piped water supply or a deep well/ cistern combination. Even the new rural houses seem to mimic the suburban pattern in which houses are lined up in rows. In the eighty-year historical reference period, access to roads seems to have become as important as access to water in house siting. John B. Stephenson described the same pattern in his study of a North Carolina mountain community (1968). In both Ridge County and Stephenson's Shiloh older structures, especially pioneer cabins, are located off the ridges and down the slopes near water, whereas new buildings are convenient to roads. Although I did not examine this pattern directly in relation to the social relationships of older people, it seems that the contemporary road-oriented house-siting pattern is consistent with the needs of older people for nearby neighbors.

Records from nearby weather stations show a humid continental climate (Daf in Koppen's classification). Mean January temperature is just above freezing and the mean July temperature is 77° F. Precipitation, averaging just over 43 inches per year, is fairly evenly distributed, although in the fall the monthly averages are slightly lower. Of course, such long-range averages obscure a fair amount of year-to-year variation. During the time I conducted my research, there was a bad drought that significantly reduced tobacco yields. Garden produce was also very limited.

Many elderly informants insist that in the early decades of this century and presumably earlier, winters were more rigorous. Snow lay on the ground longer, and no one had trouble keeping uncured or lightly cured meats in unrefrigerated, uninsulated meat houses through the winter. The affluent had sleighs before automobiles became common and roads were improved. In recent times a sleigh could have been used on only a very few days a year. Nonetheless, even a moderate snowfall can form substantial drifts in the lee of roadcuts and along the ridges, so residents are highly concerned about the possibility that transport may be interdicted. Informants worry particularly about the danger in cases where emergency medical assistance is needed, for professional medical care is far away. Parents of school-age children also fear disruption of the school bus system.

The environment presents a number of plant and animal species that can be exploited for food. Younger and middle-aged men hunt squirrels and rabbits, as well as some deer, the population of which has been increased through state government programs. Raccoons are hunted at night with packs of dogs. Fish and turtles are taken from the river and its tributaries. Papaw and various greens such as lamb's-quarter are collected, but the most popular wild plant food is blackberry. The berries are made into cobblers, pies, and jam. Occasionally young people will gather berries to sell. Jam cake made with wild blackberries is a preferred food, often prepared or purchased from skilled cooks of the neighborhood at Christmas.[1]

Ridge County has experienced a consistent pattern of demographic change since its founding in the 1860s. These changes consist of population decline, increase in average age, and transition from a pyramidal age-sex distribution to a columnar pattern (van Willigen, Arcury and Cromley 1985:51). The population pyramids of 1900 and 1980 are displayed in the figure. Like many other rural communities, Ridge County has manifested the effects of the "migration turnaround," in which "a rising rate of exodus from metropolitan areas and a declining rate of departure from nonmetropolitan locations between the 1960s and the 1970s" (Long and DeAre 1982:1112), began to increase the populations of rural communities. An important cause of this shift nationally is rural industrialization (Fisher and Mitchelson 1981, Lonsdale 1981, Wardwell 1982). Industrialization in nearby counties is a factor in Ridge County population change.

The total population of Ridge County in 1980 was 2,265 persons, a substantial decline from the 4,900 who populated the county in 1900. During this time the average age of the population changed from a median of 22.4 to 35.5 (Arcury 1983:44).

---

1. The following recipe is typical: Cream 1 cup of butter with 2 cups of light brown sugar. Add the beaten yolks of 3 eggs and beat well. Fold in a cup of blackberry jam. (Blackberry jam made from wild berries would be the ideal ingredient. The seedy, slightly bitter taste is desired.) Sift 3 1/2 cups of regular white flour. Take 1 cup of raisins and 3/4 cup of chopped nuts and roll them in 1/4 cup of the flour. Add 2 tablespoons of cocoa powder, 1 teaspoon cinnamon, and 1 teaspoon ground cloves to the flour and resift. Dissolve two teaspoons of soda in 2 cups buttermilk and add to the flour mixture in small amounts. Add nuts and raisins. Beat the whites of the 3 eggs until stiff and fold in to the mixture. Butter a nine-inch tube pan. Fill the pan and bake at 250 degrees until cake leaves side of the pan. Turn the cake out, and when it is cool frost it with traditional caramel frosting. Frosting may be prepared by melting 3/4 cup of butter to which is added 1 1/2 cups of brown sugar. Add 1/4 cup plus 2 tablespoons cream and bring to a boil. Take off the heat and let cool. Add 3 cups of powdered sugar and a teaspoon of vanilla. Beat this until it is smooth and creamy. Frost.

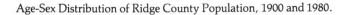

Age-Sex Distribution of Ridge County Population, 1900 and 1980.

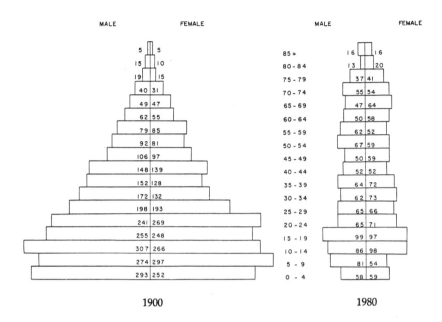

The number of persons aged sixty-five years and older per 100 children (aged under fifteen) increased dramatically, from 14.0 to 74.1 in the years between 1900 and 1980. The age-sex pyramids show the fundamental change in the population structure. The 1900 pyramid displays the triangular pattern of a growing population. The cohort of those of child-bearing age is large and the number of elderly is small. The columnar pattern of the 1980 "pyramid" indicates demographic stability and low fertility. The smaller cohorts of those 15 to 19 and 20 to 24 are produced by out-migration.

Since Ridge County (and all the rest of Kentucky) was originally part of Virginia, most of the earliest settlers were Virginians. It appears, however, that most of the pioneers who struggled over the Cumberland Gap were of Scottish and Irish antecedents, not of the English gentry, who created the traditional source of affluent elegance in Virginia before the Civil War.

Most founders of elite Kentuckian lines entered after the Revolution, many by way of the Ohio River. With them came some southeastern Pennsylvanians, including some of Germanic ancestry, as well as those of Scotch-Irish and English origin. In these original cohorts there were few Scandinavian or Mediterranean peoples. Thus the early Kentuckians were principally Scotch-Irish, with some English, and a sprinkling of Germans. Few owned black slaves. Very early in the existence of the county the black population was as high as 4 percent, but by 1980 blacks had all but disappeared, leaving the Scotch-Irish, English, and Germanic ethnicity pattern more or less intact. Recent inmigration has changed the pattern in a minor way.

Historically, the destination point of the out-of-county migration streams seems to have come closer. A review of old newspapers shows that early in this century there was substantial migration to places "out west," such as Kansas. Recently the migration has focused upon the industrial cities of the Ohio Valley, and, since the 1960s, industrial work opportunities in nearby communities. The development of these opportunities contributes to increasing demographic stability. It is important to note that stability here refers to stability of the demographic pattern, not stability of actual individuals. In other words, the population continues to churn. An important theme in discussions of the county with informants is the out-migration of young people caused by lack of jobs.

Since the county was formed its inhabitants have made their living from the land, whether as small-scale freeholders or tenants cropping on shares. It was the land and its products that provided the foundation for social life. Ridge County possessed and, to a large extent, still has what scholars of American life regard as agrarian society. The region within which the county lies has been described by Thomas D. Clark, the eminent southern historian. "Its present social organization," he writes, "represents one of the best examples of rural agrarian America to be found anywhere. It is a microcosm of the great pioneer American dream of agrarian security on the land" (1979). The core of Ridge County social and economic life, then, is the freeholding farm family.

The agrarian pattern has changed somewhat since the 1960s.

The amount of industrial employment available to Ridge Countians has increased dramatically (van Willigen, Arcury and Cromley 1985). In 1960 the majority of the labor force (63.7 percent) was employed in agriculture, and only about 4 percent in manufacturing. Twenty years later 21.7 percent of the labor force was employed in manufacturing and 24 percent in agriculture. Taken at face value, these figures seem to indicate a precipitous decline in the importance of farm employment, but this is simply not the case. First, many factory-employed Ridge Countians maintain a secondary involvement in farming. Second, it is apparent that the numbers of people involved in factory employment and share-cropping are inversely related to each other. Factory employment can be interpreted as an economic alternative for the landless. The absolute number of land-owning farm operators has not greatly declined. Third, farming is a traditionally valued activity still highly visible in the daily flow of the community. Industrial employment takes place at the end of a commuting trip.

The most frequently used farming system in Ridge County includes burley tobacco, forage crops, and beef cattle. These three agricultural commodities are the only ones produced by the majority of Ridge County farmers, but 10 percent of the farms also produce corn, milk, or eggs. Virtually no other commodities are produced for the market.

Burley tobacco is an unusual agricultural commodity in a number of ways. It remains one of the most labor-intensive crops raised by American farmers. In addition, marketing is controlled through a quota system. Although the right to sell tobacco can be leased to other growers within the county, labor intensiveness tends to limit the size of farms. Burley tobacco production is less amenable to large-scale "agribusiness" approaches to farming. The system of market quotas and price supports has evolved over the last ninety years. Before World War I and within the memory of some individuals interviewed, some farmers organized a production boycott of tobacco in an effort to raise prices in this county and others. The "Cut-Out," as it was called, though enforced by terroristic "night riders," failed to produce results in the short run. Nevertheless it is still remembered. People who are quite old recollect incidents of interfamilial conflict in the community caused by the depredations of the masked night riders. Later, out of the violence and economic chaos of this period emerged the contemporary system of price supports as part of the New Deal. The future of the program is uncertain, but at present those who own land with a market quota allotment and who choose not to grow and sell tobacco can lease their allotment to someone else within the county. The pattern across the burley belt is for lessees to be younger than the lessors, and the fee charged constitutes a useful supplementary income for older landowners.

The burley tobacco crop cycle starts in the late fall, when farmers prepare beds used for the production of seedling tobacco plants. Because this can occur before the previous year's crop is marketed, farmers often say that "tobacco takes more than a year to raise." In the early spring, after the danger of frost is past, seed is planted in the beds and fields are prepared. Beds require treatment for weeds and nematodes, accomplished in earlier times by burning wood on the beds; now, beds are almost always treated with a poisonous gas (methyl bromide). In late May and early June the young plants are transplanted or "set," with the aid of a machine originally developed for planting to- mato seedlings. Throughout the summer the tobacco is culti- vated and fertilized like any other crop, but it also needs to be topped after it sprouts some faint pink blossoms. Topping is done by hand. After topping, it is sprayed with a chemical some- times called sucker dope which inhibits the growth of stems and leaves off the main stalk. Following this operation, the leaves of the main stalk enlarge, and then the vivid green leaves slowly turn lemon-yellow gold.

In August the farmer, his family, and perhaps some hired hands harvest the mature crop stalk by stalk. Cutting tobacco is arduous work, a younger man's task done with a sharp steel blade hafted to a two-foot wooden handle and swung like an ax. The cut stalks must be impaled on sticks that allow the quickly wilting tobacco to be hung in a curing barn, or "housed," as people say. Sometimes, if clear weather is predicted, the newly cut tobacco is left in the field to take on a "good wilt." As the barn-hung tobacco is slowly cured, its color changes to various shades of brown—russet, tan, reddish brown. The barns, strategically placed to catch prevailing winds, scent the countryside with the pungent aroma of cured burley. When the crop is fully cured, it is prepared for market.

Fall and winter days are spent in the stripping room where the cured leaf is stripped from the stalks. The slow, tedious work is accompanied by entertaining banter about the quality of previous crops, gossip about public figures, and speculation about market prices. As the crop is "stripped out," it is stacked in anticipation of transport to market. Traditionally, tobacco was stripped and then tied into what were called hands, but during the course of my research, this technique was abandoned in favor of baling, which decreased labor costs. The cured leaves are simply pulled off the stalk and dumped into a press, which produces a federally approved bale. The result is less pleasing aesthetically than the hand-tied crop.

As the tobacco-production cycle unfolds, work with other crops, such as hay and corn, proceeds. Although important in their own right, these crops are less susceptible to damage from delays in the crop cycle. Moreover, with modern equipment, they can be raised by a single hand. Many farmers possess modern hay balers, which produce large thousand-pound bales that can be left in the field instead of stored under cover. Corn production is also highly mechanized. Corn is harvested either as green silage or later in the year for grain. Much of both of these crops is used on the farm as livestock feed although some is sold on the market.

Today a majority of farm operators keep cattle, mostly small commercial herds of beef cattle. About 13 percent keep milk cows. The beef cattle are fed on summer pasture grasses and hay cut several times during the season from the sloping fields. Farmers follow different strategies. Some breed and feed to market size, some breed and sell immature "feeders"; Others forgo breeding, with its risks and demanding calving period and buy feeders. These herds are managed on foot and the animals sold at various times during the year. There is a tendency to reduce herd size in the fall to avoid some feed costs. While many farmers raise beef cattle, only a few operate dairy herds. Ridge County is in the "milkshed" of Cincinnati, Ohio. In the past, large numbers of sheep were also raised, but these have all but disappeared. People attribute this transition to killer dogs. The previously ubiquitous family milk cow and hog lot have also become extremely rare, but in spite of the complete substitution of tractors for draft horses some horses are still raised for riding. These are often better-quality saddlebreds, such as Tennessee Walkers and Morgan horses.

While it is clear that agriculture is an important component of the economic life of Ridge County, its relative importance has dramatically declined since 1960, when the process of rural industrialization began to be felt in this region. As I noted, there are almost as many Ridge Countians employed in manufacturing as there are in agriculture, and typically those employed in manufacturing are younger in-migrants. The average age for those employed in farming is 37.1 years, whereas it is 26.5 years for manufacturing. About 55 percent of the manufacturing employees are in-migrants, compared to 33 percent of the agriculturally employed (van Willigen, Arcury and Cromley 1985:53). The age-sex pyramid for the manufacturing segment of the population has the triangular shape of an expanding population, but the farming segment is columnar, indicating demographic stability. These patterns are products of processes operating over the last twenty years.

During the network sample reference period, agriculture changed in a number of ways. Production intensified, for example, and market orientation increased dramatically. While it is difficult to determine ratios of subsistence product to market product, since World War I there has unquestionably been a massive shift to the market orientation. Many subsistence-oriented economic activities have been abandoned. The farms of the earliest period of the century were smaller but much more diverse enterprises than the present farms. Agricultural census statistics reveal substantial change in the pattern of commodities produced during the network sample reference period. Formerly, a wide variety of agricultural commodities was produced for the market, including sheep, oats, barley, wheat, rye, soybeans, honey, many kinds of orchard fruits and berries, and swine. Now such commodities are no longer produced, or they are produced in minute quantities. What remains is an intensified production system oriented toward the market.

The decade of the 1930s brought great change to Ridge County. The quality of roads improved. Many more autos and tractors appeared. The town and some rural areas were electrified. Later, chemical fertilizers increased yields in tobacco and other crops. Before these fertilizers were introduced farmers used crop rotation and fallowing to preserve soil fertility. Tobacco is very demanding of soil nutrients. Farmers preferred to put their crop of burley on "new ground" or if they were near the river, on "overflow ground" fertilized by the deposits of alluvium. The use of fertilizer resulted in radical increases in yields per acre in this important cash crop, and these increases necessitated changes in the market quota system used to support prices.

Nowadays, Ridge County households are provisioned largely by periodic trips to the grocery store. People prefer to travel to nearby towns, where the stores have lower prices and greater variety. The country stores are treated like the convenience stores of an urban area. Patrons stop in for a loaf of light bread or some pop. The storekeeper may make sandwiches for farmhands and passers-by at dinnertime. The stores in town are similar, though their inventories are somewhat larger. During the childhoods of the people in my sample who grew up in rural Ridge County there was much less use of stores. There have been stores in the county since it was founded, but earlier stores carried relatively few groceries. Local farmers visited these stores infrequently, the older people report. In the 1930s some of the rural neighborhoods were served by huckster trucks, often called stores on wheels, whose drivers would both buy and sell. They carried such groceries as canned goods, flour, sugar, and coffee and would buy small amounts of such farm produce as chickens and eggs, keeping accounts of the transactions, which were settled up from time to time. Many of the large variety of commodities produced could be purchased outside of stores too. Cans of surplus cream were sold at the "cream stations" for example, and some farmers sold homemade sausage door-to-door in town.

The transfer of personal and real property at the death of a Ridge Countian is structured by state and federal law as well as local custom. The only lawyer in the county seat estimates that about half the people leave a will, and most of those probated on smaller estates in the county leave everything to the surviving spouse. Settlement of the estate is delayed when a person dies intestate. Usually the estate is divided equally between spouse and children, with some contingencies if such heirs do not exist. Under the federal tax exemption of $500,000 in effect during the research period, Ridge County estates were exempt and spouses could inherit without paying tax. The lawyer estimated that typical estates ranged in value from ten to thirty thousand dollars. The largest approached a hundred thousand dollars. Some in the county transfer property to their children in anticipation of death, but this strategy is not common because the tax advantages are very limited. Inheritance practices have changed somewhat through the years. In early wills a farm was often left to the wife for her lifetime only; at her death the property would pass to the eldest son or the sons. Wills in the past frequently settled cash on daughters in lieu of land.

As in most complex rural communities, the social organization of Ridge County draws much of its substance from kinship, coresidence, and association. Kinship relations are expressed in the narrow sense of nuclear families raised in a single household but also in a larger framework of "my relatives." Coresidence and kinship are expressed in household structures. Propinquity of residence is an important basis of neighborly relationships. The county itself is a kind of coresidence-based social organization. Affiliation of another type develops through association in clubs, cooperatives, and churches. Sometimes relationships developed because of kinship, coresidence, and association become especially close and perhaps intimate, and these are regarded as friendships.

Any Ridge Countian will tell you that kinship is important. Residents will often say, "Here, everyone is related." If pressed they might also say, "Kinship is important for many people but not all" and "Kinship is less important than it used to be." I found strong evidence that the kinship system has changed; population changes have reduced the number of related people living in the county.

Kinship implies special kinds of relationships of support and collaboration, many of them across different age categories. Support is expressed in many ways, and these relationships exist in two frameworks: the relationship itself and community recognition of the relationship. Kin ties require a kind of general collaboration on the part of at least a portion of the community. Collaboration can be based on sanction against improper behavior and support of proper behavior. Kinship binds an individual to the history of a particular family because families have reputations. I will return to it in a later chapter.

Neighbors, linked by shared interests based on propinquity, also relate to each other in special ways. The role of neighbor, like that of kin, follows a prototype based on cooperation. The relationship is less close and more materially based than kinship, and it does not require the same community collaboration. People largely know who is related to whom, and they take family ties into account in their actions. They are less aware of neighborly relationships. Historically, the basis of neighborliness was economic collaboration, sharing work for efficiency and economy of scale as well as the noneconomic benefit of sociability. Neighbors joined each other for barn raisings, wood cutting, animal butchering, wheat threshing, cornhusking, sorghum molasses making, fish trapping, and the like.

It is the economic basis of collaboration that has changed more than anything else. Virtually none of these tasks are now shared by neighbors. Agricultural work may be shared, but only infrequently. The reasons for these changes are complex. First, many of these activities are rarely done today, cooperatively or not. When they are done the means have become more technical than social. Capital is substituted for social organization in many cases. For example, in the past, neighborhood or kin groups formed what were called meat companies, cooperatively purchasing cattle during the warmer months, butchering it as needed, and sharing it out. Such a system was needed to overcome the storage problem. Pigs were never part of it because there was a ready way of preserving pork by curing it with salt and sugar. The system has now given way to freezers and custom butchers.

The diversity that used to exist in farming also encouraged work sharing. Nowadays, however, neighbors may not be farming in the same way, and work sharing is less attractive. Moreover, in many cases more neighbors now work in manufacturing and are not farming at all.

Most Ridge Countians belong to voluntary associations, including sports teams, service clubs, secret lodges, professional associations, school associations, educational organizations, and various others. The number of voluntary associations within the county increased dramatically during the network sample reference period. Federally supported rural development efforts from the New Deal onward often were expressed in clubs, such as 4-H and homemaker clubs. One striking change in voluntary associations is the proliferation of age-graded associations. Earlier in this century organizations were mostly for adult males. Trends started in the 1930s produced more associations for younger people, and the number of organizations for women increased to some extent. Most recently the number of organizations for older people has also increased.

Ridge Countians are introduced to clubs quite early in their socialization. Many have their earliest affiliation with a clublike organization in their Sunday school classes, which often have an officership, dues collection, and a program of activities outside of class. They also encounter voluntary associations in school. Perhaps because of the church experience, nearly all the voluntary associations have some religious content in their activities, however minor. Typical are the arrangements found in homemakers' clubs, in which one member is designated "devotions chairman." It is usual for meetings of associations to start with prayer.

Of course, Ridge County is more than a terrain serving as a platform for socioeconomic activities. It is a political community. In most of United States, particularly in predominantly rural areas, the county is a social unit as well as a political division. The county seat, which is political center and first link to larger entities—district, state and nation—is often the local commercial and educational center and the site of major social events. This is especially true of the Commonwealth of Kentucky, where the county political functions, brought by early settlers from Virginia, resulted in a proliferation of counties, from the original three to the present-day 120 (Ireland 1972:2). The political consciousness of the settlers and the difficulties of travel to a distant county seat in the late eighteenth and the nineteenth centuries seem to have encouraged this pattern. Once established, each new county became a focus of interest and a basis for self-identification of its inhabitants. Historically, rural Kentuckians tended to identify very strongly with their counties. The historian Robert M. Ireland notes, "Originally intended to be but subdivisions of the state and, as such, her agents in local affairs, most of Kentucky's counties had become semi-autonomous by the mid-nineteenth century, deriving a fierce loyalty from their residents. Rivalries between counties could be as intense as those between states" (1976:2). The sense of affiliation has changed with time because of transformation in the economy, transportation, market organization, and education. It seems to community members that the sense of affiliation with the county is less important than it was thirty years ago, when the county seat played a more central role in the marketing of agricultural produce. Nevertheless, rural Kentuckians still have a strong identification with their counties.

In some ways this pattern resembles the intracultural ties of peasants and tribal peoples, who may see their world categorized into a "we" versus "they" dichotomy. The few bits of historical information we have found on the formation of new Kentucky counties suggest that there must have been high tension at the time, but once a new county was legally constituted, it quickly became the focus of affect. As Ireland expresses it, "Kentuckians have always taken great pride in their counties. This was especially true before 1900 when most Kentuckians lived on farms or in rural towns and villages and owed their greatest allegiance to local institutions such as family, church, political parties, and state and local government. In an age of relative immobility, 'home' had a more permanent and meaningful hold on the hearts and minds of Kentuckians. And for most Kentuckians, "home" meant one's own county rather than his own town or village" (1976:1). Yet, although scholars and citizens would agree that the county can be interpreted as a social unit, the social affiliation implied is weak. In the case of Ridge County, with its small population and area, one might expect the ties to be relatively strong. Certainly in the past Ridge Countians had substantial opportunity for face-to-face contact. One of the best opportunities was provided by the "court days," on which the circuit judge would hold court in the county seat. Court days were also market days and people would come to town to sell farm produce and shop.[2]

The focus of political life in Kentucky counties is the courthouse and the school board office. Ridge County is no exception. Because the county is small, its political life has a decidedly local focus. Statewide office seekers have relatively little to gain by currying the favor of Ridge County officials, and therefore they wield little power regionally. Whatever regional influence they possess is based on coalitions between Ridge County and other smaller counties in opposition to more heavily populated areas. This pattern is expressed in regional rather than state contexts, however. In spite of Ridge County's political marginality, some statewide candidates show up in the county seat to electioneer.

The formal political organization of the county consists of the county fiscal court, a legislative body equivalent to what is called the board of supervisors in other areas. The court is composed of five magistrates, elected from magisterial districts, and it is headed by the judge of the fiscal court, elected at large. The title *judge* has been retained from an earlier usage. Actually, the incumbent in this office is the chief executive officer of the county. This organizational pattern is English in origin, introduced to Kentucky through Virginia (Ireland 1972).

A primary administrative concern of the court since statehood has been the roads. The small budget of the county does not yield much opportunity for self-serving behavior on the part of political leaders.

The other dimension of political life is party organization. Throughout the history of Ridge County the Democratic party has dominated local political offices, and the number of Republicans has been small. People seem tenacious in their party loyalty, and many Ridge County Democrats would accept the appellation "yellow dog Democrat," a term sometimes used in traditional Kentucky party politics to describe a person so in-

2. A colorful description of a court day in a nearby town can be found in James Lane Allen, "County Court Day in Kentucky," *Harper's Magazine* 79:383-99 (1889). The scheduling of court days, which rotated from county seat to county seat in a circuit, resembled that of the "solar markets" of Mesoamerica.

tensely loyal to the party that he or she would vote for a yellow dog if it was a Democrat. The local Democratic organization is relatively closed. New residents are unable to assume positions of authority in the party organization. Older party members past retirement age maintain substantial power after they have reduced their involvement in the formal organization of the party. They are still consulted, and their advice is heeded. Formal leadership is held by somewhat younger males, in their fifties and sixties. The Republican party organization is very small and does not provide a competitive alternative to the Democrats. The relative strength and weakness of the two parties is historically related to political divisions developed during the Civil War, or, as it is referred to locally, the War between the States. The Republicans are historically linked to the Union side, and owing to its border-state status, Kentucky has both traditionally Republican and Democratic counties.

Politically, Kentucky is highly subdivided. There has been some talk about county reconsolidation, but the politics of that process seem so difficult that no program has emerged. What has occurred is the development of quasi-governmental multicounty planning bodies. These Area Development Districts are important to us because they are involved with the acquisition of funds for various federal programs to benefit older people, some of them funded through the Older Americans Act of 1965. Noteworthy among these programs is funding that allows the staffing of a hot lunch and recreation program in the county seat of Ridge County. This program is administered through a regional community action agency headquartered in another county.

Older people are important to the political process. As I noted in discussing demographics, the population of the county includes a relatively large number of older people, whose votes are sometimes targeted by election campaigns. Candidates for district or state offices who come to the county usually show up at the Senior Citizens Center, where they distribute their matchbooks or emery boards to build name recognition. In this small, quiet county the center is the place where the largest number of voting citizens is congregated during the week, and transportation available at the center makes it possible to convey people to public political meetings and other activities in the region.

Administrators seem to view attendance of older people at such meetings as reciprocation for the services they receive from the programs.

Political actions of governments that impinge on the lives of older people as well as the rest of the population are manifested in two ways. First, older people show concern about political decisions. When the governor decided to close a state highway maintenance garage in the county, for example, older people worried about the ability of the road department to keep roads clear of snow in the winter so that those with medical emergencies could get to the doctor or hospital. While the issue was current the garage closure was mentioned in prayers offered at church. The strong concern of old people was presumably matched by that of factory workers who had to commute to other counties and dairymen dependent on the milk pickup. This research did not attempt to assess the political awareness of older people, but observers did not note any diminution of awareness with age. Older people continued to be concerned about the future of Social Security, curtailment of services offered at the Senior Citizens Center, decisions concerning government programs dealing with tobacco production, and other political issues. To make a purely subjective observation, older people in this county seem to have a higher level of political awareness than younger people.

To an extent, the lives of older people are shaped by government law and regulation. Most apparent are the economic benefits of Social Security or Medicare legislation. There is also legislation that benefits older people through special programs, like those provided through the Older Americans Act. Also relevant are the state laws that structure inheritance. Outside of the body of regulation and law specifically related to older people are numerous other laws and regulations that affect older people indirectly. Among the many examples is the legislation that facilitated industrialization in nonmetropolitan areas, which tended to reverse the steady flow of population out of the rural areas of the country. Out-migrants have always tended to be younger. The regulations dealing with agricultural commodity marketing have also affected the lives of older people. In the 1960s, for example, dairy farmers were required to upgrade their milk-handling equipment to improve sanitation. Because the newly required equipment was expensive, the new regulations produced an extensive, largely age-stratified shakeout of dairy producers. More older farmers than young ones decided not to make the additional investment in bulk refrigeration equipment, probably because they were less able to justify the investment in view of their shorter future, which would not allow sufficient discounting of the cost of the equipment. Older farmers usually simplified their operations or retired.

Religious life in Ridge county is expressed in the activities of thirteen churches. The churches manifest similarities and differences in their organization, theology, and congregations. Viewed from a national perspective, the differences in theological orientation may seem minor. From a community perspective, however, certain theological distinctions appear to serve as key symbolic differences between churches. They are important and well understood. The churches represent a number of coherent religious traditions, but the term *denomination* does not apply very well, for participants in the largest religious tradition, the Christian Church, deny that they represent a denomination. The religious traditions represented include the Christian church, the Methodist church, the Baptist church, the Christian-Baptist church, Assembly of God, and a locally organized Holiness church. Typically these churches offer Bible school classes Sunday morning for all ages at ten o'clock and worship at eleven. Most also schedule worship services for Sunday night and one weekday evening, usually Wednesday. There are some exceptions to the pattern; the locally organized Holiness church meets only on Saturday night, thus avoiding direct competition with other churches. This is a typical pattern for new churches, which allows people to attend the new church without actually leaving the old church.

Although conversation between people about religious matters tends to focus on differences in theology, ritual, and organization, there are a number of fundamental similarities among the religious beliefs of these people. All the churches are Protestant, and all profess the divinity of Christ. Although there are many nonbelievers, or at least nonchurchgoers, there are no non-Christians and virtually no Catholics. In this framework the Protestant/non-Protestant contrast is not especially important. All the churches also share a commitment to evangelism. All are concerned with "winning souls to Christ," and all support missionary work. The dominant theology is Arminianism, stressing the idea of individual volition and the establishment of a personal relationship with God. None of the churches accepts the doctrine of predestination or the elect. They emphasize a faith-based salvation rather than good works. In an urban context, all these churches would be regarded as fundamentalist in their view of Scripture. Yet there are variations in the degree of interpretive flexibility allowed, and the differences are sufficiently clear to local residents so that the member of one county church can refer to another church as fundamentalist.

The differences among churches are subject to two contradictory processes. One is the identification of key symbolic differences in belief and practice, which are apparently used to represent the differences between churches. That is, while the differences may be systematic, a limited array is identified and used both within and outside a church to signify different affiliations. The second process involves difference reduction, which primarily occurs where there is flexibility of practice in ritual. If there is choice, people tend to choose the least different alternative. For example, the Methodists allow members to choose pouring, sprinkling, or immersion baptism. All other churches practice immersion, regarding the other forms as insufficient to secure salvation and eternal life. Individual Methodists tend to choose immersion, thus making their practice congruent with other churches. Through these kinds of processes there emerges a community theology. Not only is there a tendency for theological differences to be deemphasized, but a number of other practices seem to have the effect of reducing competition between churches. There appears to be very little proselytizing, for example, among churchgoers affiliated with another church. Virtually no effort is made to have people change affiliations. Churches make a considerable effort in scheduling revivals and vacation Bible schools to avoid competition. In the town churches vacation Bible schools are apparently coordinated so that children can attend the entire succession of programs at the different churches. The coordination appears best between the non-Holiness churches. There is also evidence that when new preachers are hired in the churches with congregational structures, the members of the pulpit committee will screen out applicants who are overzealous about proselytizing. Despite those culturally acceptable limits on competition, however, church growth is important, and membership can decline quickly. Those that were growing seemed to be those with good preaching or recreational youth programs. Church leaders emphasize the need to grow in order to prevent decline.

The clearest contrast in theological orientation is between churches with a Holiness orientation and those that are not Holiness, but there are no widely used community labels for this contrast, no terms for what I am calling non-Holiness, for example, although members of Holiness churches might be called Holy Rollers by members of the other churches. One significant theological contrast between Holiness and non-Holiness churches is the doctrine of salvation. Salvation, of course, is the state in which a person is able to have a continual blissful existence in the spirit world. To simplify, the mainline churches require sincere confession and correctly administered baptism for salvation, but the Holiness churches add a third requirement, variously expressed, involving a merging of the person with the "Holy Ghost." This condition can only be achieved through the efforts of the person. The mainline churches recognize this process but see it as something that occurs in a limited sense with confession and baptism. In these churches, once you are baptized, you are saved. In the Holiness churches, once you are baptized, you are ready to be converted. The mainline approach has a contractual quality about it. As a mainline preacher said, "It's more cut and dried." The most visible effect of this contrast is in the worship service. Holiness church services contain less prescribed ritual and more apparent improvisation. The style of worship is more animated. Overly formal preachers may be criticized for "binding the meeting." Often worshipers exhibit dissociative states that are taken as evidence of the "infilling of the Holy Spirit." There are some differences among the Holiness people, as well. Some proscribe "speaking in tongues;" in other churches it is common. The frequency of dissociative states is quite variable.

Churches are important in the social lives of older people in this county, and church participation increases with age. The highest level of church affiliation in the county is in the 65-69 age stratum. Many of the churches provide special services for older people, which seem to be valued. Church services are important sources of information about friends and neighbors. It is important to remember that these churches are very small and do not have the resources to offer elaborate services. Average attendance for the largest of the churches in the county is about 120. Only about a third have fulltime preachers.

During the reference period of this study there have been some changes in the religious life of the community. Perhaps the most important has been the advent of Holiness churches, all but one of which date from the late 1950s. The sole exception is one very recent, very small church initiated by a local house painter and handyman. The special services for older people are another innovation. Many churches now practice visitation or make tape recordings of the Sunday service available to church members who need to stay home. At least one church has an active program of field trips for older people, which they enjoy a great deal. During the reference period there has been little change in the content of worship and beliefs. Styles of preaching are somewhat different. There is less reference to the consequences of sin and more content related to social relationships. That is, preachers engage in less "hell-scared preaching" and more "love preaching," stressing Christian ethics. Congregations are said to be less intimidated by hell-scared preaching than they used to be. They have become "gospel hard." Yet overall, religious life is stable. As one ninety-year old woman said in response to a question about change in worship in her church, "The Bible hasn't changed, has it."

Religion in Ridge County is the religion of the Protestant Reformation. Many of the transformations that emerged in fifteenth-century European Christianity are still emphasized in discourse and ritual. Perhaps most important is the idea of a faith-based salvation unmediated by a priest and independent of the requirement for "good works." These ideas are expressed in liturgy and in song. Everyone has access to eternal life and the capacity to enter God's Kingdom.

When Edmund Leach, the social anthropologist, wrote, "Every real society is a process in time" (1954), he was describing the relationship between formal social structure and behavioral alternatives, not the totality of relationships between individuals, groups, and the environment. Nevertheless, his simple declaration prepares us for an expanded perspective consistent with the goals of this study. Cultural processes are both recurrent and directional (Vogt 1960). In this research I am concerned with a recurrent process—social interaction—and a directional process—social change.

It is useful to consider the total process of community change through the concept of ecological transition, which consists of changes in the relationship between humans and nature. John Bennett defines it as the "progressive incorporation of Nature into human frames of reference" (1976:3). We are most concerned with the sociological implications of this process, including increased scale of society, development of hierarchy, concentration of wealth and power, and the breakdown of local self-sufficiency (Bennett 1976:6). In addition, the fact that these phenomena are operating at various system levels is as important to us as it is difficult to parcel out. There are important events outside the community that are not accounted for in detail. I am concerned with old people interacting with those around them now, but in order to understand that interaction it is necessary to think in terms of transformation from the past and changing relations with other levels in the total system. The difference between then and now or there and here is never as clear as it seems.

Expressing understanding of the ecological transition of Ridge County requires a serial discussion of several processes, equivalent to the facets of the idea developed by John Bennett, which are components of the same general process and reflect nationwide transformations. In previous usage, the process would be referred to as modernization.

During the period of study, between 1900 and the present, the foundations of the total process of ecological transition are agricultural intensification and market penetration. Agricultural intensification is usually taken to mean any change that increases agricultural productivity. In Ridge County increases in agricultural productivity were associated with increased use of off-farm energy sources and decreased diversity of farm products. There has also been delocalization, that is, an increased reliance on energy obtained from outside the community (Pelto 1973), as well as parallel increases in market penetration. In other words, there was a shift from production for consumption to production for the market, or commoditization of production. Increasing government regulation encouraged simplification of the farming system. Most noteworthy in this regard are the changes in sanitation requirements for dairy and meat products, which reduced the complexity of farms in the sense of reducing the range of commodities produced. Processing of meat products for sale virtually ceased, although sausage and ham making still continues in some households for domestic consumption. Dairy production was transformed from a ubiquitous sideline to an infrequent specialty.

Throughout this eighty-year period there was a more or less constant decline in population, related to an increase in farm size and increases in work opportunities in the industrial North. The migration changed the age structure of the population from the pyramidal structure of a young and growing population to that of an older, mature population with a lower fertility rate (van Willigen, Arcury and Cromley 1984; Arcury 1984).

The evidence for the working of these changes is ubiquitous in American rural life. Yet apparently there is substantial variation between different regions in the United States. Ridge County retains many of the attributes of older days in spite of the substantial change.

3. Collecting Data

Vernon: In the years past, say fifteen to twenty years ago, he'd hire a bunch of young boys . . . and put up his own hay and enough to feed his cattle. In the past ten years, you can't hardly get it done. *John*: So it's not so much having to do with him getting older, it was just the shortage of labor. Vernon: That's part of it. And him getting old too. He had tractors and all like that, but he would mow his own . . . keep his land cleaned off, you know, and do that kind of work but he wasn't able to put up his hay and he wasn't able to get help to do it. So he kinda had to be buying most of his hay in the last few years. *John*: Do you find that older farmers will buy more of their hay? *Vernon*: Yeah, lot of them have to, unless they can get some young man to put it up on the shares. *John*: Hmm . . .

Vernon: And now, some older people have gone this way, John, especially older people who have a sum of money. Instead of keeping cows all winter, they'll go in the spring and buy a bunch of young calves, say three hundred to four hundred pounds. *John*: In other words you go from a breeding operation to a feeding operation? *Vernon*: That's right. Only not a feedlot feed, just a pasture feed. *John*: And your requirements for hay and all that would be less. *Vernon*: Wouldn't have to worry about hay. Lot of the aged people have gone to doing it that way. For one thing a piece of land in this country without cattle on it soon goes back to the Indians. It just grows up, you know. And if you got land you need some cattle on it. *John*: Just to keep it clean? *Vernon*: That's right. But the shortage of help. . . . See, years ago, a man could on any house on any corner pick up a young man who'd help him feed cows. But that's hard to do nowadays. *John*: What are they doing? *Vernon*: Working in factories.

This short portion of an interview reflects a typical data collection event, a free-ranging interview with a farmer about his views on the adaptations of older farmers. The information obtained represents one kind of data used in the analysis. The goals of this research required a wide variety of data-collection techniques, including participant observation, key informant interviewing, structured network interviewing, and content analysis. The many kinds of data collected can be classified into the commonly used social science categories, quantitative and qualitative. These often-used labels conveniently gloss over differences within the categories and important similarities across them. It may be more useful to think in terms of a single, very complex category, ethnographic data, some of which is numeric and some textual. This chapter briefly describes how the ethnography was done. Of all the techniques used, social network data collection is discussed in relatively greater detail because there is somewhat less documentation of such techniques in the literature and my techniques deviate to an extent from those used by others. In general, my treatment of network data collection consists of an extension of Sokolovsky's excellent "Network Methodologies in the Study of Aging" (1985), and the ethnographic process is consistent with the mode described by *Anthropological Research: The Structure of Inquiry* (Pelto and Pelto 1978) and *Training Manual in Policy Ethnography* (van Willigen and DeWalt 1985).

Ethnographic data obtained through participant observation, key informant interviewing, and the reading of documents were especially important for initial discovery and subsequent interpretation. Philip Drucker and I were mainly responsible for this aspect of data collection, and our efforts were somewhat complementary. Drucker, in his seventies when the field data were being collected, was more readily able to establish rapport with older members of the community. Furthermore, he had substantial practical knowledge of animal husbandry and agronomy, which paralleled much important knowledge of the community, and he had experience working in rural Kentucky. For my part, I was better informed about religion and federal programs as they related to community life. We operated in somewhat different circles. Drucker tended to participate in occasions where men congregate to gossip, reminisce, and exchange information. I developed relationships with people I met at church and those I did farm work with.

We relied principally on the time-honored procedure of key informant interviewing in the field, finding, like many ethnographers before us, that persons of good will vary in their ability to organize their experiences into meaningful accounts. We tended to spend more time with people who could tell their stories well. Some of the interviews were tape recorded, and of course, notes were also taken. In brief encounters and occasional gossipy sessions, where note taking was not appropriate, the ethnographers listened and wrote notes afterwards.

Much of our interviewing was aimed at establishing a data base for the reconstruction of about eighty years of culture history, and such interviews are subject to important limitations. Perhaps the most important is the impossibility of cross-checking interview data with direct observation. We made some use of newspaper files to compensate for this difficulty. Many informants found discussing life in the past very satisfying, and often the interviews contained segments of what R.N. Butler referred to as life review (1963). The experience of the interview became very important to some informants. We decided to share some of the interviews about life in the past with the community by placing audio tapes of interviews in the public library and writing stories for the local newspaper on historical topics.

Participant observation was an important aspect of the research strategy. We participated in and observed a variety of activities. We attended church; visited the Senior Citizens Center; did agricultural labor, attended community festivals, sporting events, and trials; and went calling, in addition to engaging in all the routine errands and activities of daily life—shopping, picking up the mail, going to the library, and the like.

Church attendance led to more intense participation in church life. I spent time working on church renovation projects, visiting shut-ins and the sick, and attending Bible class. I also participated in most of the agricultural operations associated with the dominant crop, tobacco, as well as other tasks.

While we relied heavily on oral testimony for our historical reconstruction, local newspapers provided an invaluable supplement. In a sense they "split the difference" between the rather bland statistical sources, represented by the United States Census, and the rich personal nature of oral testimony. Newspapers are most useful for providing rather precise documentation of the changing patterns of scheduling the ceremonial cycle; the history of formal community organizations, including dates of club formation and the initiation of various government programs; and innovations in agricultural production and marketing. We were pleased with the results achieved by using newspapers and oral testimony in tandem. Each source stimulated inquiry into the other domain and allowed for continual cross verification. Historical documents like the newspapers help elucidate the processes that have produced the structure of contemporary life. As David C. Pitt notes, "During his research the anthropologist or sociologist only sees or surveys the social structure and culture at a given point in time and space. But this structure is part of a historical continuity" (1972:3).

One effect of historical change is the creation of differences in the way people describe reality, based on differences in their experiences. These differences in historical experiences have been discussed within the conceptual framework of life-course theory (see esp. Elder 1974, 1987). Thomas A. Arcury has analyzed life-course transitions in the Ridge County elderly population between 1900 and 1980 (1986). Old people, because they have longer histories in the community, have experienced a greater share of the change that has occurred in Ridge County, with significant effect on certain kinds of self-reported data. When research subjects are asked to assess community-level changes subjectively, as was done in some ethnographic interviews, accounts derived from various age cohorts will vary for at least two reasons. The first is that the segment of cultural knowledge reported by an age cohort will vary because of the differences in the adaptation of that particular age cohort, which is to say that the lives of older people and younger people are to some extent different because they "need" to be different. Persons of different ages use different adaptations; therefore, the knowledge they use also differs to some extent. If we define culture in a non-configurationist sense, the differences can be said to be cultural, but although they may be quite significant I do not feel it is necessarily productive to talk about age cohort "subcultures." The term is imprecise, and it is certainly possible to argue that the various age groups all draw their reported cultural knowledge from the same font. Second, and more important from the perspective of this set of issues, in subjectively assessing cultural transformations in their own culture, people tend to employ comparisons that were operating during previous times of their lives. Thus an older informant will perceive a contrast, where a younger one will not. In the realm of social organization, for example, younger informants are much less aware of the general patterns of network density reduction in the community, whereas an older informant will typically note that most people used to "know everybody else" and that this is no longer the case. Out-migration and in-migration have resulted in the loss of known people and the addition of unknown people to the social field. The same phenomenon is manifested in the area of age segregation. Younger informants tend to report a low level of age segregation, comparing the situation in Ridge County to a depiction of urban life, with its higher reliance on nursing homes. Older informants, however, report the contrast between the period of their early enculturation and the present, and they perceive a greater contrast between current reality and the mental or cognitive ground of their understanding. A vivid glimpse of the relationship between perception and experience of an older person living in a community similar to Ridge County can be found in Wendell Berry's novel *The Memory of Old Jack* (1974).

We must also ask what effect cohort experience has on self-reports. We did not directly attempt to assess change in the network interview and therefore do not have to deal with this problem directly. It was especially apparent in the ancillary discussions of exchange behavior.

There were, of course, some biases in our ethnographic information. We have data from more male than female informants, though precise count is not possible because of some informal group interviews. An early concern that differential longevity of males and females might create a bias proved of little consequence; demographic data indicate that age cohorts of males and females are roughly equal. Male and female knowledge is somewhat different. The difference varies from generation to generation but may be greatest among the older people we spent so much time interviewing. Very many women throughout our ethnographic time horizon and even before, we were told, actively participated in the crop-production cycles and hence were well informed about it. Nevertheless, their knowledge of crop and livestock production was more generalized than that of men. Their knowledge of livestock management, other than caring for newborn lambs and calves, tended to be quite limited. Butchering of hogs, lambs and cattle was a male specialty, also, as was the handling of meat, especially the curing of hams and bacon. Women were knowledgeable about food preparation, meal planning, and maintaining household accounts. Their knowledge of the historical transformations of food preservation was especially good. Men tended to have very little apparent knowledge about food preparation. Most can prepare a meal of sorts in an emergency, but they know little of the culinary arts, except in one area: preparation of fish and game is special male province. Women were better informed about recent federal programs for older people. Male and female speech patterns, especially in use of four-letter vulgarisms, differ too, although some differences are associated with social class. An important source of bias, especially in historical reconstruction, is the apparent differential migration of people in terms of class differences. Tenant farmers come and go, some buy land and stay on. Oral reconstruction tends to be done with the people who had reason to stay.

Differing compliance with standards of the value system governing interpersonal relationships is another potential source of bias in a special way. In our field research it became clear that the situational context of the ethnographer's first encounters with knowledgeable informants had an effect on the type of responses to queries and volunteered statements. An experienced ethnographer can create bias through, among other things, participant observation. Informants can be expected to associate ethnographers with the activities and institutions in which they participate, and the association determines whom the researcher can interview and, to an extent, the content of the interview. Philip Drucker and I were associated with somewhat different segments of the community, I largely with the churchgoers and he with the unchurched or "lost." In any case our participation was well spread in Ridge County society because of data collected through a house-to-house survey and the random selection of persons to be interviewed in the network component of the study. General ethnographic interviewing and participation focused on the mainstream of life in Ridge County, the community of Christian, freeholding agriculturalists, both male and female.

The ethnographic data were recorded on file cards and coded using a much-modified version of the *Outline of Cultural Materials* (Murdock et al. 1971) perhaps the most widely used code for ethnographic materials. The method employs three-digit codes, which can be used to retrieve content in sets of ethnographic field notes. This particular system possessed some drawbacks, but a ready-made code also has some advantages. Each individual data record card carried a serial number, data, topical heading, and notation of recorder's identity. Field notes were recorded as soon after the observation or interview as possible.

The technique used for observing networks was developed for this project. In any consideration of network concepts it is important to emphasize that the interrelationships between concept and measurement are not uniformly developed. The discontinuity between concept and measurement usually consists of the elaboration and development of conceptualizations of network variables that are beyond the analyst's capacity to measure. As D. Heckathorn expresses it, "Field studies typically generate huge volumes of data which cannot be accommodated within formal models; and formal models may demand enormous volumes of data which are nearly impossible to gather in the field" (1979:223). Most typically the constraints on measurement are practical rather than theoretical. Valid and reliable measurements could be designed, but they would be too costly to administer or too tedious for subjects.

In choosing an approach to measurement, it is necessary to consider the research questions, the technical knowledge of the researcher, and resource limitations, as well as other factors. One difficulty to be overcome is a lack of documentation of the specific measurement procedures used to produce the empirical literature. In the late 1970s some researchers began to address this problem. Most noteworthy among them is Sokolovsky, whose work provided the foundation for this discussion.

The many ways of conceptualizing the general network concept can provide some choices to the network analyst, but sometimes the choice is more apparent than real. Practical considerations intervene in a number of dimensions. Some techniques are only useful under certain special circumstances. Others are more widely applicable.

The network analyst's first choice is whether to study virtual networks or the various proxies for networks. Much of the social gerontology literature measures network proxies, including such constructs as social interaction (Lowenthal 1968; Tesch, Whitbourne and Nehrke 1981) social space (Clark and Anderson 1967), sociability (Wagner 1960), social isolation (Lowenthal 1968), social integration (Rosow 1967), and social participation (Graney 1975; Pihlblad and Adams 1972; Zborowski and Eyde 1962). Some of this research uses more straightforward measures, such as relationship counts (Norman, et al. 1982). There are also many studies that purport to focus on network but use such a low level of conceptualization that they are outside the purview of network analysis.

Without engaging in a thorough analysis I would like to point out some fundamental contrasts between the virtual approaches and the proxies. A contrastive feature of networks is that they are complex, real units; they exist in reality. Although they lack some attributes of groups, being unnamed, without boundary and noncorporate, they exist socially at a supraindividual level. They are an example of what Boissevain (1968) calls a nongroup. The proxy measures are more abstract than the network measures. They are analytical constructs, which are not typically the focus of research except as independent variables. Thus they are more attractive to researchers. But social networks can be plausibly analyzed as either independent or dependent variables. In this research networks are treated as a dependent variable.

It is possible in network studies to use the entire network of a social entity as the unit of analysis in what is called the whole network strategy (Craven and Wellman 1973, Sokolovsky and Cohen 1978). The alternative is the personal approach, in which data is collected from the perspective of the individual. Both approaches allow the study of individuals in a network context, but whole network studies are quite rare and are usually limited to studies of "small clearly bounded populations" (Sokolovsky and Cohen 1978:327). Peter Killworth and H. Russell Bernard used the whole network approach to study a small prison (1974).

They asked research subjects to identify those with whom they had contact from a deck of cards on which the names of all inmates were placed. Roster data collection procedures are somewhat problematic in natural community settings, however, because of the size of the roster required. This type of research is especially useful in studying communication networks within groups allowing very detailed analysis. They are most useful where group boundaries and membership are quite clear. The data produced can be analyzed in a number of ways suggested by the mathematics of graph theory (Berkowitz 1982, Hage and Harary 1983, Knoke and Kuklinski 1982). The personal network approach, on the other hand, permits sampling of larger populations and consideration of many more variables.

The researcher must also decide whether to study active or potential networks, that is, actual existing network linkages or the network that can be reached though existing relationships. The concept is very useful for thinking about how networks are activated, but measurement of potential networks is difficult. "For practical methodological purposes," Sokolovsky proposes "that *behaviorally* active linkages be the focus for empirical comparison while not ignoring the cultural meaning of potential networks for understanding the adaptation to old age" (1985:5).

For the most part, measurement in network analysis is based on self-reports, and the researcher must therefore use informant cognition as a proxy for behavior (Killworth and Bernard 1976:270). Researchers use self-report measures because direct observation is expensive and intrusive, but research testing the difference between reported and observed social networks has shown that the two measurement strategies produce substantially different results. The work of H. Russell Bernard and Peter D. Killworth is especially noteworthy in this regard (Bernard and Killworth 1977, Bernard, Killworth, and Sailer 1980, 1981, 1982; Killworth and Bernard 1976, 1979). They examined a number of communication networks in which it was possible to compare reported data with observed. In one case they investigated social networks of deaf persons who communicated within their networks using teletypes. It was found that their self-reports of interaction frequency contrasted substantially with data on interaction derived from teletype hard-copy records of interaction.

The researchers examined other data with similar results and concluded, "We are now convinced that cognitive data about communication cannot be used as a proxy for the equivalent behavioral data. This one fundamental conclusion has occurred systematically with a variety of treatments, all as kind to the data as possible. We must therefore recommend unreservedly that any conclusion drawn from the data gathered by the question 'Who do you talk to' are of no use in understanding the social structure of communication" (Bernard, Killworth, and Sailer 1980:28).

Others have also examined this problem, from a variety of perspectives (Knoke and Kuklinski 1982;30-33; Burt and Bittner 1981; Freeman, Romney and Freeman 1987). Some have asserted that the special properties of the populations they studied obviated the problem. More interesting is the recent work of Linton C. Freeman, A. Kimball Romney, and Sue C. Freeman, which views informant accuracy from the standpoint of the psychology of memory organization (1987:311). This work supported the conclusion that "inaccuracy" in recall was biased toward the long-term pattern. That is, patterns of reality were exaggerated through the inaccuracy: the important was emphasized, the unimportant dropped. An individual's mental structure of a particular phenomenon is developed out of experience and is reflected in recall. The conclusion, if generalized to the network data collection I am reporting, is that recall inaccuracy would be biased in favor of the informants' underlying mental image of their social world. The task posed to the respondents in the study of Ridge County was implicitly focused on determining the underlying pattern rather than specific events. That is, they were asked not who did you speak with this week but who do you speak with as often as weekly. I have no reason to believe that either Bernard, Killworth, and Sailer or Freeman, Romney, and Freeman are wrong. There is no question that the reality being studied is a socially constructed reality. Still, studies of observed networks will continue to be largely limited to circumstances and populations where there are naturally occurring hard records.

Social network analysis usually involves limiting the network in some way. Researchers do not observe all conceivable extant links, they select, whether for practical or conceptual reasons.

It is often necessary to limit the scope of the inquiry in order to reduce the cost of interviewing. Also researchers may want to focus their attention on certain kinds of relationships. In any case, social network research virtually always focuses on truncated networks. Data collection requires that the subject's network be limited by the criteria used to list network alters. Subsequent to listing, other data are usually collected on the listed individuals. The basic approaches to collection vary in terms of their initial listing criteria, which might be a specific time period, interaction sector, or level of importance or frequency of interaction. A comparison of these approaches will be made shortly.

To summarize, social network researchers must choose the kind of networks that they are going to analyze. They must select direct or proxy measures, personal or whole network perspectives, active or potential interactions, reported or observed networks, and truncated or entire networks. In actual practice, the choice is quite limited. The social network and aging literature appears to be almost exclusively focused on personal, active, reported, truncated networks. Social networks are but one approach to the measurement of the social lives of older people; from a network perspective there are many proxy measures available. Beyond this the researcher may select which network variables to measure, which research population to interview, and the extent of ethnographic contextualizing. All the studies to be compared in Chapter 7 reported research on directly measured, personal, active, reported, truncated networks, but they manifest substantial differences in approach nonetheless.

Despite the similarities in networks analyzed, there is, unfortunately, no one dominant technique for the collection of network data, even though network data seem to be very sensitive to the effect of the technique used. Among the technical alternatives for collecting this kind of data is the Network Serial Method, developed by Roger Sanjek for the collection of network data in Accra, Ghana (1978:257). Based, according to Sanjek, on the work of A.L. Epstein (1969), the technique produces "documentation of an actor's spatial movements and interactions over a relatively short sample period of time" (Sanjek 1978:258). The Network Serial Method is a method for exploring direct, personal, active, reported, truncated networks using a time period as the basic listing criterion. Data are collected through relatively unstructured interviews (Sanjek used two) that take place at the residence or work place of the ego. Sanjek's interviews were about "the course of events from the earliest morning activities until bedtime" (Sanjek 1978:259), and after the interview a "narrative version" was constructed (Sanjek 1978:260). The data recorded in the narrative are divided into the constituent "multiactor scenes," a concept derived from Marvin Harris (1964:94-99). Various alter, scene, and activity characteristics were coded. The alters were coded by sex, ethnicity, kinship relationship to ego, age status (i.e. child or adult), and social class (based on occupation). The activities at each scene were also coded.

Sanjek suggests that the basic approach could easily be modified to suit the context and goals of the research. For example, the technique could be adapted to a telephone interview or diary approach. He also suggests that the approach could be used with direct observation instead of self-reports. Certainly the variable measured could be adjusted to a variety of research goals.

Another approach, the Catij Method, involves the use of a card-sorting task with research subjects (Bernard and Killworth 1973; Killworth and Bernard 1974). Research subjects are given a deck of cards upon which the names of a group of people are written. The group can be as large as 150. The respondent is asked to sort the cards into four categories: "(1) those with whom he/she has *a lot* of communication; (2) *some* communication; (3) *hardly any* communication; and (4) *no* communication" (Killworth and Bernard 1974:337). The data collected in this way is used to construct a matrix thought to represent communication links within a group. They can be processed to depict group relationships as well as individual. The approach is most suitable for enclosed groups, such as prison populations. The Catij Method depicts direct, active, and reported networks. In contrast to most other techniques, the approach yields information about both personal and whole networks. Although the data on each individual is limited, linkage identification is not truncated, for such roster techniques involve lists of potential alters.

The Psychosocial Inventory Method is a profiling technique developed by E. Mansell Pattison (1977; Pattison, Francisco, and Wood 1975). It produces data that can be classified as direct, personal, active, reported and truncated. The listing criterion used to inventory the network is subjective importance (Pattison 1977: 230). The respondent is asked to "List by first names or initials all persons who are important in your life at this moment, *whether you like them or not.* The respondent is told that the persons listed can be related in any way; they can be "family members, relatives, friends, neighbors, workmates, clergy, bosses, recreational associates, etc." (Pattison n.d.:1). Each relationship is then rated by the research subject in terms of frequency of interaction, strength of feelings toward the alter, frequency of emotional support, pattern of change in the relationship, intensity of relationship, content of support relationships, spatial proximity, and symmetry. The interview schedule is best understood not as a research instrument but as a screening/diagnostic device leading to therapeutic counseling. The data collected with a form are supplemented with some diagraming of relationships done by the subject-cum-patient. The subjective importance listing criterion truncates the network list. In the course of the interview "connections" between alters are identified.

Jay Sokolovsky developed the Network Profile Method, which was used in three of the studies I have selected for comparison. In addition to the two studies done by Sokolovsky and Cohen (1981, Cohen and Sokolovsky 1978), Kevin Eckert used a modified version of the technique to research relocated elderly people in southern California (1983). Like the Network Serial Method, this method is direct, personal, active, reported, and truncated. It differs in using "sectors of interaction" to list network alters. The interview attempts to identify all those individuals the ego interacts with in a given setting. In the single resident occupancy study, Sokolovsky identified those alters with whom the ego interacted at the hotel, as well as other "sectors of interaction."

Sokolovsky's profiling method is based on a simple interviewing strategy that involves engaging the ego in discussion of the people they have contact with in their social world, subdivided into the "sectors of interaction." The sectors of interaction would, of course, vary from population to population, and different eliciting frames would therefore be used in different studies. The sectors of interaction in the SRO network study included hotel residents, informal support system outside the hotel, hotel staff, and public agencies/caring professions (Sokolovsky 1985:19). After the alters associated with the different sectors are listed, the researcher proceeds to obtain data on the relationship, which can comprise several variables. Sokolovsky speaks of "member attributes" such as age, sex, address, ethnicity, and occupation, and "linkage attributes," including variables characterizing interaction and exchange.

Questions about interaction focused upon duration of the relationship, frequency of interaction, typical time and place of meeting, and time of last contact, among other things. A number of questions explore exchange transactions, asking about conversation content, money lending, food and meal sharing. Interviewers also asked whether the alter was regarded as a friend.

In the SRO study, Sokolovsky used frequency of interaction as a secondary limiter. He notes, "I included only links active within the prior year (known for at least a month) with a minimum frequency of once a month for hotel residents, once every three months for non-residents, and once a year for kin" (1985:20). Persons that interacted less than that were thought to have "little practical or cultural/psychological meaning to SRO residents" (1985:20).

The Network Profile Method represents a useful and easily adapted technique for network data collection. The general framework of sectors of interaction is applicable in a variety of situations. The technique would, of course, not be standardized from setting to setting because the relevant sectors of interaction would vary from study to study. The technique should only be used after substantial ethnographic data collection, including participant observation experiences. In use, like the Network Serial Method, it is relatively informal and uses simple instrumentation.

All but the Catij approach use the same basic principle. The researcher provides a conceptual frame such as a place, a time period, a social category, or a degree of emotional importance to the research subject and then asks the subject to provide the names of the people with whom they interact. The listing is supplemented by questions dealing with a variety of attributes of the ego, the relationship and interaction and the alter. Data are collected through interviews, diary keeping or questionnaires. The anthropologists seem to argue for substantial ethnographic inquiry before details of the question content are specified. It seems likely that these general characteristics of network data collection will be maintained in the future. The innovative data collection procedures developed by Bernard and Killworth seem applicable in only a limited number of special situations, but the issues they have raised are useful to understanding the work being done using more conventional techniques.

The Kentucky Exchange Network Inventory (KENI), developed for this research project, resembles the methods developed by Sokolovsky, Pattison, and Sanjek in providing a conceptual framework and then asking the research subject to list names of people with whom s/he interacts. Like the Network Profile, Network Serial, and Psycho-social Kinship approaches, KENI produces a data record that directly measures active, personal, truncated networks through self-reports. The major difference between KENI and the other techniques is the listing criterion, frequency of interaction (subjects were asked who they saw every day). Moreover, there are differences in the variables measured following the construction of the list and the operationalizations used for the variables.

The core of the interview task was the compilation of a list of the people with whom the research subject spoke. The interviewer started the interview by telling the subject, "We are trying to find out more about people's social relationships as they grow older. You could help us very much by telling me the names of all the people you usually talk to. These people can be neighbors, friends, relatives, people you work with, fellow members of organizations or anybody else you talk to. We will ask you a few questions about these people." The questions that produced this list were geared to frequency categories. (The interview schedule and interview instructions are reproduced in the Appendix.)

The interview site was the person's home, chosen because I felt that using a standard context would tend to stimulate a pattern response, that is, that the environment of the interview would provide cues for the person's memory. Perhaps the ideal context would have been some "neutral" site, but there were none available. Therefore the only reasonable site was the person's home. The instructions specified that the interviews should not be carried out at any other place, for another location might stimulate listing of the persons the subject knew from that context.

The interviewers were told not to rush the interview. They were free to engage in lines of questioning that were consistent with other related research questions. This instruction was intended to reduce the tension of the interview situation. The discussion of the questions could be "worked into" comfortably. While this process seemed to produce relatively little additional ethnographic information, it did seem to make the interview process more interesting for both participants, probably functioning in the same way as Sokolovsky's suggestion to vary the order of the questions (1985:22). Most additional useful information produced from this supplementary discourse had to do with aspects of the relationship. The length of the interviews was quite variable. Some took less than one hour; others went on for four or five.

The frame of reference was the person's typical experience, not a specific period of time. The general question was "Who do you see," not "Who did you see this past week (or in any other time period)." To ensure a certain minimal level of intimacy, the interviewer was to list only those for whom the research subject knew the first and last name.

There were other minimum criteria for listing, as well. Conversation had to go beyond mere spoken greetings. Such interactional encounters as listening to a preacher give a sermon were not to be counted as network links. A brief conversation between that same person and that same preacher at the close of the service would count, however. Operationally we listed any interaction in which both participants spoke more than simple greetings. Interaction by telephone was acceptable. These conditions were specified before data collection, but in fact, interviewers did not report that these specifications ever came into play to determine whether a person should be listed as part of a network.

As I noted earlier, the interview experience suggested that research subjects remembered people they liked better than those they did not like. In one case a subject did not want to name a person because the subject did not like that person. It was tacit recognition that this person was part of the subject's network. The questions were all very concrete. They did not focus upon feelings, sentiments or attitudes to any great extent. Only a question on "importance" of network ties carried a projective tone. The words used specifically referred to concrete reality and were as objective as possible. Further, the questions made sense to the respondents. Of course what was measured was not reality so much as mental images of reality.

This research purports to measure people's cognition of interaction and not their interaction. It therefore falls squarely in the mainstream of standard social network research and social gerontology. It may be appropriate to establish the concept of cognitive network and actual network, or reported and observed, to recognize their different qualities. Moreover, we need to recognize that the difference between reported and observed is not a kind of error but a distinction between the cultural world (de Laguna 1960:777) and objective reality. What we mean by cognitive network are those people the research subject perceives as within the subject's social network. That is, reporting is a function of knowing. Knowing is a function of a complex set of factors having to do with the nature of one's memory, the effect of recent experience, and the way one deals with evidence.

The questions that produced the network listing were ordered in terms of four frequency categories: daily, more than once a week but not every day, once a week and once a month. The subject was asked, "First tell me the names of the people you are likely to talk to every day, either face-to-face or by phone. I will put their names on this list." Next, the interviewer asked, "Now tell me the names of the people you talk to more than once a week but not every day" then "at least once a week," and "at least once a month." I pilot tested an earlier version of the interview schedule in which the listing criteria were social categories, such as kin, friend, neighbor, and the like. With this procedure, I found, there was a tendency for interviewees to "fill the space." That is, people tended to try to come up with names to "adequately fill" each category presented. Of course, the meanings associated with the categories do not transfer well cross-culturally, not to mention intraculturally. The concept of neighbor in a high-density town settlement pattern may be different from that found in a low-density rural setting. Some researchers are beginning to discuss the problems associated with the idea of friend, for example. Claude S. Fischer effectively demonstrates some of the characteristics of persons labeled friends in a northern California sample but makes the point that the concept is used indifferently by researchers (1982). The frequency categorization proved workable and had the effect of eliminating a complex cognitive stimulus at the outset of the interview that would have produced a significant cultural bias, on the one hand, and a limiting mental set, on the other. Frequency categories seem to bear few preconceived meanings. Whereas we often think of friends or neighbors as a category, we never think of "those we see once a month." The frequency listing criteria has more potential cross-cultural use than the sectors of interaction of the Network Profile Method (Sokolovsky 1985). The network records produced using the social categories were significantly larger than those produced using the frequency category approach.

Following the listing of network alters the informant was asked to categorize the alters, nonexclusively, as relatives, co-workers, fellow members of organizations, neighbors, and friends. There was no difficulty with this procedure on the surface, but it was apparent that church membership should have been separated from membership in other organizations. The meanings associated with belonging to clubs and church are radically different. The problems caused by this inappropriate lumping are minimized by having the network listed according to frequency criteria before categorization of alters.

The next eighteen items in the interview schedule tap various kinds of exchange relationships. Matched reciprocal pairs seemed to cover most of the different types of exchange that were apparent to us in observing social life. The persons were asked if they gave or took meals, gifts of food and drink, gifts, care when sick, employment opportunities, work without pay, shopping, loans of money, and loans of things. It is important to note that these were expressed as reciprocal pairs.

The item list was constructed by means of substantial ethnographic data collection. The items are based upon a great deal of experience within the community through key informant interviews and participant observation. Most of the reciprocal exchange relationships were directly observed, and the researchers engaged in many of these relationships.

There are two interesting patterns in the response to the questions. First the interview experience revealed that the selection of exchange categories was essentially appropriate. The behaviors listed in the interview schedule effectively delineated the range of behaviors that formed the naturally occurring systems of social supports in a reciprocal framework. What this set of questions apparently measured were differences in exchange patterns by age, not of life-course changes. The design is of course cross-sectional and not longitudinal. Here we can speak only of age differences and not life-course changes. In addition, based on the ethnographic data, we can speak of secular changes. Many research subjects would comment that their current exchange relationships were different from those in the past. They attributed these differences to both individual changes related to age and changes in community practice. The presentation of historical data, therefore, is most important to the analysis.

Although our list of exchange categories was apparently "complete" and culturally appropriate, we did have difficulty with one item, the borrowing of money. Undoubtedly, monetary loans are an important mechanism of exchange, but the response from subjects was strongly negative. Since this item seemed to put a strain on the respondent beyond its utility for analysis, we dropped the question. This was the only troublesome item among the exchange questions. Interestingly, the question on borrowing and lending "things" was not associated with the same problems. Financial transactions, however, were viewed as none of our business.

The interview schedule required two explicit evaluations. First, the respondent was asked to identify his or her best friend. Some were reluctant to pick out one person as special. A similar problem developed with an item that asked the respondent to rate the importance of the alters. For this a card was presented on which were drawn stairsteps numbered one through five. Prominently displayed with digit one was the label "least important" and with the number five, "most important." Some people found this evaluation difficult. They "solved" the problem by assigning the "most important" score to all members of their network. Most respondents had less trouble. The task seemed more difficult for respondents who were less experienced with testing.

The research reported here used varied ethnographic data derived from participant observation, key informant interviewing, content analysis, and network data collection. The data were related to each other in developing the procedures for collecting network data and in the final interpretation.

Network data collection employed a technique developed for this study, the Kentucky Exchange Network Inventory, which uses frequency of interaction as the listing criterion. This technique may have a higher potential for use in comparative studies than other techniques because frequency categories are connotatively neutral. The frequency category approach, of course, would not work where people did not have equivalent time categories. Nevertheless, standardization of collection technique would bear significant advantages for researchers attempting to understand the social life of older people.

4. Farm, Family and Homeplace

Two of them sat solidly in the stubble of brown grass above the pond. The third, Lewis, was fixing to stand, and he began to stretch out his gangly frame. They were there to watch Billy Elliot clean Johnny Tolliver's pond with his bulldozer. Lewis had just finished picking the last of the green peppers that he had encouraged his grandkids to raise to help pay for college. The peppers had done the kids some good; most were sold under a contract in a nearby town. Lewis had picked a last bushel for his wife to can and freeze, although he thought they still had some left over from last year. Stiff from the bending, he stood to stretch. Virgil and Johnny, both heavier, sat upright about forty feet above the pond. They could feel the dampness underneath the thick mat of fescue and other pasture grasses. Not that they ever thought of it, but Lewis, Johnny, and Virgil had known each other for about sixty years. It would have been easy for them to figure out exactly when they had met, for they first got to know each other when they all started school. They were waiting in the late October sun for Billy to finish his maintenance walk-around on the D6 Caterpillar bulldozer he'd trucked down from Riverton.

After greasing a fitting Billy took his place on the well-worn seat of the D6, jiggled the hand levers, and rotated the ignition switch to the right. The warm engine coughed and then clattered alive. All three enjoyed being around Billy, and Johnny had finally got him to come clean the pond on his farm. Billy had slowly worked the jobs between here and Riverton, building farm ponds and doing other bulldozer work, hauling that old yellow Cat on its lowboy trailer. Billy had a way with most everything. All his family were dead honest and hardworking. He was a master with that Cat, working the earth in a delicate and respectful way. With him you never had to keep track of his hours, he'd tell you exactly the number of hours he had worked.

They all nodded when Virgil said, "Ol' Billy, he's a good'n." Lewis responded, "When did you ask him to work this pond?" After a pause, Johnny said he had asked him in spring. Billy is a deacon at the Riverton Christian Church and is on the cemetery board there, where most of Johnny's mother's people are buried. Johnny went to decorate the graves last Memorial Day half thinking he would arrange for the bulldozer work. Billy, he knew, would be there trying to raise money from the visitors to help the cemetery pay for that summer's grass cutting. Anyway, almost six months later Billy had worked through all the farm jobs between Riverton and Johnny's pond.

Lewis, Virgil, and Johnny saw each other regularly—two, three times a week. Their meetings always seemed to have a practical purpose, however trivial—borrowing tools, finding someone to lease their tobacco allotment, or asking one another about a blighted garden plant—always something having to do with making a living. They almost never just went to see each other. Johnny's wife was dead, but Lewis's wife and Virgil's would both softly smile when their husbands would explain that they were going over to the store or some such thing. They had all known for three weeks that Billy was going to clean out the pond today, so this gathering had been planned for a while. Lewis, at least, had come to arrange with Billy to do some work for them. Virgil had put half a sack of turnips in the bed of his pickup to share out with his friends. All of them got out of the house much more than their wives did, but they always offered an explanation.

Needless to say, Lewis, Virgil, and Johnny are members of each other's networks; these kinds of encounters are the substance of part of their social lives. It is essential to remind ourselves of such scenes as we try to understand this aspect of aging. In this chapter I will be discussing some properties of the networks reported to us by the people interviewed. Networks are people in relationships. Here are described the people whose networks were examined and those with whom they had social relationships. A sample of older people was drawn and data were collected on those people with whom they talked.

Those interviewed were selected randomly from a subset of the entire county population, consisting of a listing of all households that contained persons sixty years of age or older. Interviewers were instructed to ask first about the willingness of the specific sampled person to be interviewed but if necessary to substitute any other resident in the household sixty years of age or older; this usually meant the spouse but on occasion a child or other relative. The sample represents 33 percent of the population sixty and above and 40 percent of the households in which persons in that age category live. The sample includes 139 persons, 65 males and 74 females.

For analysis the sample was divided into five age groups, more or less equal in size: 20 percent were aged 60 to 64; 22 percent were 65 to 69; 18 percent were 70 to 74; 20 percent were 75 to 79; and 20 percent were 80 and above. The mean age of the sample was 72.6 and the range was 60 to 97.[1] Approximately 47 percent of the sample was male and 54 percent was female. The mean number of years of school attendance was 8.7. People of these ages living in this place typically left school at the end of eighth grade. The median is eight years. About 40 percent of those sampled had eight years of education. About one-fourth of the population had twelve or more years of education, including some college work.

In Ridge County, as in the United States as a whole, the population of active farmers has become old. As I noted in discussing demographics, Ridge County consists of a younger population that relies on industrial employment often mixed with some farming and an older population of farm operators with little involvement in industrial employment. This pattern is reflected in the occupations of those interviewed; for both men and women, farm backgrounds are typical.

The distribution of occupations among the persons interviewed was examined from two perspectives: current occupation

1. The median age was 72 years and the standard deviation is 8.13. The distribution appears normal but displays some boundary effects in the youngest end of the distribution. The sampling was not stratified according to age.

and occupation at retirement. Almost half those interviewed regarded themselves as retired; 11 percent considered themselves farmers; 10 percent reported nonfarm occupations; and about 30 percent reported themselves as housewives. Of the persons reporting themselves as retired about 47 percent were farmers; 72 percent of all males, retired and non-retired, were farmers. The remainder reported a variety of non-farm occupations. There was a higher proportion of retired people in the sample than in the general population of this age and fewer persons with non-farm occupations. The farmer and housewife categories are more or less comparable. Being a housewife on a farm entails a great deal of agricultural labor and most certainly involves participation in farm management and decision making. In this community, where there is a high level of involvement in farming, the boundary line between working and retirement is quite vague. It is important to note that the respondents themselves applied the label "retired."

Many farmers withdraw only gradually from active involvement in farming. Even late in life they will participate in management decisions, even though they present themselves in an interview as retired. Their decisions will be expressed through their tenants or people to whom they have leased their tobacco marketing quota.

It is apparent that as farm operators age their goals change, resulting in transformations in the farming system they employ. Aging-related factors in farm management include the physical capacity of the farm operator to work, the decreasing availability of future time within which investments can be justified (amortized, consumed, worn out) and the special needs associated with passing the farm on to someone else.

Physical stress can be reduced by hiring more work out on a custom or cash basis; purchasing rather than raising animal feed; eliminating certain crops or livestock; and recruiting others to raise the crop on shares. Another possibility is investment in labor-saving equipment, but such purchases are made only reluctantly because older farmers may feel that they cannot get sufficient use out of a piece of equipment. The introduction of new technology often represents a dilemma for older farmers. If they are "set in their ways," it is largely for economic reasons. Older farmers can manage to do some "work off a tractor," even though they may be less fit, but they often feel there is no time to pay for and depreciate expensive equipment.

A major constraint older farmers face is the shortage of rural labor characteristic of most of Kentucky. They are very sensitive to labor shortages because of their need to hire people to substitute for their own labor. Frequently hiring occurs through networks. For example, the children of a neighbor might be hired to put up hay. A source of labor may keep a farmer involved in farming activities later in life.

The special needs associated with divestment involve farm practices that keep the buildings fit and the fields clear. Building maintenance necessitates prevention of theft and vandalism, in addition to painting, roofing, and other activities. Keeping the farm clean-looking becomes a very difficult problem for many older farmers. Beef cattle help achieve that goal. Some farmers will raise a few head of cattle primarily to keep pastures clean and just to stay involved. Some express the idea that not growing something on the land is wasteful. One woman reported that she was able to keep cattle on the farm with the help of her neighbors for fifteen years after her husband died; for her, a farm without cattle was "just throwed away," and she said "It's a shame not to have anything on it."

There are ways to make livestock raising more compatible with aging. Farmers can improve the tractability of their herds by selective breeding. Angus cattle are reputed to be easy to handle. Ease in calving is also an important consideration because of the savings in veterinary costs and the reduction in stressful labor that comes at inopportune times. Ease in calving, however, has a cost. The calves are small and therefore less valuable. The lack of growth potential may result in a discounted price when they are taken to market.

No matter what strategy they use, as farmers age they are able to invest less time in maintenance, which is lower in priority than production. As a consequence their farms may be subject to comment. An interesting consequence of the aging process is that farms of older farmers tend to grow up in brush and therefore to provide better habitat for wildlife. It is likely that the rabbit population is related in some way to the average age of the farmers in specific counties. Farmers use large rotary mowers, known as Bushhogs, to keep land clear. To hire someone

to mow would present an extra cost not directly related to production. A similar pattern is associated with lawn care in both
town and country. Some people highly value the appearance of
their yards. As they become less capable of operating a lawn-
mower they will try to hire someone to mow; some are able to
find help through kin networks. Not being able to adequately
maintain the appearance of the yard may be pivotal in deciding
to move.

The fact that the agricultural economy is based upon tobacco
is also important for our analysis. Tobacco is a labor-intensive
crop that requires many separate tasks, some difficult, some
easy, in terms of the physical stresses they place on the body.
I spent many hours at every task in the production process, from
"burnin' beds" (preparing a tobacco seed bed) to assisting in
"makin' a basket" (preparing a sales unit of tobacco) on a sales
warehouse floor. Without any measurement other than participant observation and key informant interviewing, I was able to
determine in a general sense the age structuring of specific tasks
in tobacco production. The point is that even very early in the
career of a tobacco farmer he is deciding to spend money for
wages instead of using his own personal labor for stressful
or dangerous tasks. Without working capital or family labor
resources, the farmer may have to maintain a more broad-
spectrum involvement in agricultural labor. These decisions are
adaptations to age, and they begin very early in a person's farming career. To state the principle in general terms, it is as if in
response to the aging process farmers begin to substitute cash
and social credit for their own labor. Frequently they may withdraw more or less totally from the entire production process,
merely collaborating with the person who is "raisin' their 'bacca
on the shares."

Even after they stop working on the farm, older farmers, as
the owners of capital, have many opportunities to participate in
farming through the management decisions associated with
renting out land, barns, and marketing quotas. In the realm of
tobacco production the farmer may move into town and rent the
farm to a tenant who lives on the land. The tenant may use the
opportunity to work toward becoming a farm owner. In share-
cropping the tenant often does not live on the farm. The image
of the poor sharecropper does not apply very well to this cate-

gory of farmers. Many undoubtedly are faced with real difficulty, but others who crop on the shares simply use the arrangement to expand already large operations. They may farm their own land and rent more acreage from others. Land may also be used by another farmer for "money rent." The landowners retain the right to market a certain number of pounds of tobacco a year, whether or not they produce the tobacco themselves. Under the provisions of the long-standing federal tobacco program, the right to market a quota can be leased for the season. The cost varies according to market price and production levels the year before as well as other factors. Thus, most older farmers derive income from market quota leasing of tobacco and engage in these relatively simple business transactions with those who lease their quotas. These lease arrangements may be with larger-scale producers who want to add to the production on their own farms or leased land. Older farmers will also rent out their tobacco curing barns. Until the land is divested, the farmer continues to participate in an annual cycle of management decisions, which may result in relationships with tenants. The complexity of the institution of tenancy in United States agriculture is effectively depicted by Miriam J. Wells in a recent publication (1987). Her analysis shows that tenancy can be a function of life-cycle or production expansion as well as a manifestation of economic marginality.

For farm housewives the demarcation between working life and retirement is especially vague. Women seem comfortable reporting themselves as retired even though they are rather involved in farm management decisions. Although retired farm housewives spend less time in actual farm activities, they carry the core of their work load, "homemaking," until they simply cannot do it any more. Because of differences in the nature of the labor and the way work is allocated to males and females in this community, women contribute valuable labor to the household longer than men do. Even if farming stops, someone must still cook, clean house, and wash clothes. Men do not do such work very frequently when they are young and they do not tend to embrace it as they age. Women do try to simplify homemaking activities by reducing the size of gardens and the amount of food preservation and closing off part of the house. They may use more prepared foods, and the family may eat more Sunday dinners out. But in general, a woman continues to keep house, and if her husband dies, she also takes over management decisions concerning tobacco sharecropping and rental and lease arrangements. She may have help from a son, a tenant, or someone else who simply manages the farm.

In the area of work and occupation there is a significant potential for cohort effects because of rapidly changing circumstances of employment. Opportunities for industrial employment have been very limited for most of the study period. In the last twenty years there have been some increases in opportunities for industrial employment. The effects of this change are not as apparent as they will be in the future.

The persons interviewed live in various parts of the county. Somewhat over half live in higher-density settlements, such as the county seat or the few rural villages. The remaining individuals live in small residence clusters or on isolated farmsteads. The distribution of settlement as it relates to age is an interesting topic itself. As people grow older in this county, there is a strong tendency for them to move to town. They need to be nearer available services such as the bank, social services offices, and the post office. There also seems to be a need to escape the isolation of rural life. Often there is concern about the older person's ability to drive. Those who can drive can get around and meet their needs with minimum trouble. As the ability to drive declines, people become more dependent on other people, less and less able to control the amount of time they spend in contact with other people. As they become more limited in their ability to use a car, they move to town where they can get around on foot. The county seat has a substantial number of older people living in it. A group of preachers mentioned in conversation that they thought of the county seat as a kind of retirement community because of the high concentration of older people. One stretch of the main street has come to be called widow's row. Relatively few of the women living there are able to drive.

Interviewers asked a number of simple questions related to capacity and resources for communication—whether the respondent owned a car, had a license to drive, had a telephone. In addition, the egos were asked if they had any physical impairment (see Table 1).

Males were significantly more likely to own cars and be li-

Table 1. Individual Communication Resources

	Attribute Sample		Male		Female		
	Percentage	N	Percentage	N	Percentage	N	Prob.
Car	61	84	82	53	43	31	.0001
License	54	74	66	49	34	25	.0001
Telephone	83	113	75	48	90	65	.0177
Impairment	41	57	54	31	46	26	.1331

censed drivers than were females. Both car ownership and licensure decline with age, but not significantly. Men seemed to
keep their driver's licenses even if they did not drive. Nevertheless, the decline in licensure is greater than that of car ownership, because, perhaps, their cars were driven by others.

The frequencies associated with automobile transport need to
be interpreted in historical terms. Over 30 percent of the sample
were born before cars were common in the region; the first one
sighted by an informant was seen in 1904. Even so, few cars
were in use for the next twenty years. It was not until the 1920s
that the first car dealership opened in the county. Thus every
person in the sample was born before automobiles were in widespread use. Furthermore, for many years driving automobiles
was a predominantly male activity. The first motor vehicles were
cars and trucks; tractors did not come into widespread use until
later. Some informants retired from farming without ever own-
ing a tractor.

There is also a significant difference between males and
females in regard to telephone ownership. Most of us take
telephones for granted, but there are a number of rural areas
of Ridge County that did not get telephone service until the
early 1960s. Now there appears to be no difference in frequency of telephones between town and country dwellers.
The percentage of persons with telephones goes up with age,
but not significantly. Many persons maintain relationships by
telephone.

It should be noted that older persons are faced with residential
alternatives. Some move to Florida. Others move in with relatives. And there are also nursing homes or so-called minihomes,

neither of which are considered attractive. Frequently older people express the idea that moving into a nursing home is unacceptable to them. It's hardly surprising, as the nearest nursing homes are in other counties. The long-term residents of these facilities are viewed with pity, for arranging to enter such a place involves placing yourself at the discretion of other people, divesting yourself of material culture, reducing interaction with the network of friends and kin, and entering into a relationship of dependence. As one older woman interpreted the problem, "I have observed this about people that go to nursing homes. . . . when they are taken from their original surroundings, and put in a place where they have no relationship with their surrounds, their minds go . . . .I'm surrounded by things that are memories of my previous life. And if they were taken away from me, why, . . . probably my mind would go too."

Attitudes toward "rest homes" may be based on the historical prototypes, the "county poor farm," or "infirmary." In responding to a query about historical changes in the relationship between young and old, one woman said, "I suspect the thing that impresses me most [about the way old people were treated in the old days] was if you had a parent that needed care you took care of them. Nobody was sent to a nursing home. There were no nursing homes and the closest hospital was [45 miles away]." Those who had no means of support went to the "infirmary," whose facilities consisted of a number of board-and-batten houses, each comprising two rooms in a "shotgun" arrangement. These were clustered around the farmhouse of the person who had the county contract. Residents were fed from the kitchen of the farmhouse, according to the still-living daughter of the woman who managed the place from about 1914 to 1928. The diet, she said, was identical to that of the family and based largely upon foods raised in fields and gardens of the household. One male informant described the poor farm:

> That was a pretty sad thing, but it used to be the only way to take care of the real poor old people, and the simpleminded. I don't think they were supposed to keep the simpleminded ones there, but there was no other place for them—the nonviolent ones, of course. There was this lady, had a farm out on the ridge. . . . She had a big house, with

ten or twelve shacks behind it. The county offered the contract every year, and she was always the lowest bidder.
She done all right with it, though; she managed real well
and fed them good. Whenever you went there, she'd insist
you stay for dinner, an she'd give you the same food [as
she gave the residents]. It was always a real good meal,
not fancy but good tasting. But the shacks were not in very
good shape—that was the bad part.

The county contracted with two doctors in town to provide medical attention on an on-call basis.

Clearly the image of this place was negative, but not because
of the meager accommodations afforded the inmates, which
were probably not all that different from those in a typical farm
household of that period. One informant bridled when I referred
to the place as the poor farm. "Poor farm," she said, "we called
it the county home. There were many poor farms in the county."
What people objected to most was the dependency of the residents. In order to be admitted, it was necessary to go through
a public hearing before a judge of the fiscal court.

At present, the state funds "minihomes," contracting with
individuals to provide residential care in their own homes for
older people unable to live on their own. These facilities are
hardly used by the older people of the community. Most residents, if not all, were from other counties, referred through a
statewide allocation system, which places older people in the
care of the paraprofessional minihome contractors in different
communities. Planners often stress that they are "local alternatives to nursing homes" or that these homes allow people to
"stay in the community." In Ridge County, however, most residents are from other places and have very little to do with the
community social networks. Indeed, perhaps the primary benefit of such homes is in establishing a sort of social service cottage
industry. They play a useful role in the regionwide system of
care for older people, but they do not clearly function for local
people as a transitional step from independence at home, to care
by relatives, to minihome care in the community, to nursing
home care, and finally to acute care in hospital.

Some individuals with sufficient resources may move away,
most typically to Florida. Some leave altogether, selling their

homes and farms; others migrate seasonally between a home in Florida and the farm in Ridge County. Some of this group have someone manage their farms on a share basis, which usually entails simplifying the farm operation to some extent. Typically those who move to Florida go to places where others persons from the county have previously moved. There are towns on both the east and west coasts of Florida with clusters of people who hark from Ridge County. Networks are used to establish such retirement residences outside the county.

Altogether, those we interviewed reported interaction with about 3500 alters, of which 48 percent were male and 52 percent were female. Samplewide, 63 percent of the alters were the same sex as the ego. Beyond gender, the interview did not require the egos to classify the alters in exclusive categories. Thus, a person regarded as kin by the ego could also be classified as co-worker or friend.[2] About 40 percent of the alters were classed as kin, and the egos may have other kin as well, for relatives seen less frequently than monthly would not appear in the person's network as reported here. A third of the alters lived outside the county. About 30 percent were classified as neighbors. Clearly the idea of neighbor included the notions of both propinquity and "neighborliness," and some neighbors reported in the networks seem to have been people who used to live nearby and continued to interact with the ego. Certainly the listing included some former neighbors and others who had neighborly relations without necessarily living near. Only 6 percent of the alters were classified as co-workers, but this percentage may grow in the future as young factory workers age. Inasmuch as the great majority of my sample were either self-employed farmers or housewives, it is not surprising that there are relatively few relationships of this type. About 20 percent of the network

2. I chose this approach because it preserves the ego's perspective better than forced choices. I do not argue that these categories are truly emic; nevertheless, they are quite consistent with the extensive ethnographic observations I am presenting. These categories are naturalistic subsets of an implied heuristic category "persons the ego talks with at least once a month." This nonexclusive approach allows one to preserve individual and community meanings. It also tends to diminish differences between categories in the analysis.

alters were "fellow members of organizations." The most frequent classification was friend, which included 90 percent of the
alters. Best friends amounted to 5 percent of the alters.

As to the listing criterion, frequency of interaction, the egos
reported 16 percent of the alters were in daily interaction. About
30 percent were in less than daily interaction but more than
weekly; 23 percent were in weekly interaction; and 30 percent
were in monthly interaction. It is likely that there are alters that
are important to the egos who interacted with the egos less than
once a month and so were not reported as part of the networks.
It is also possible that some egos listed significant but low-
frequency alters because they wanted to include them.

Each ego was asked to rate the importance of the alters on a
five-point scale. About 39 percent of the alters were rated at the
highest level, 24 percent at level four, 18 percent at level three,
9 percent at level two, and 7 percent at the lowest level. The
scores may or may not relate to "actual importance." There is
some evidence that egos were unwilling to rank people at the
lower levels, believing that a low ranking conveyed disapproval.
It is worth noting here that relationships in this community are
very dense. I speculated that in a community that was less dense
there would be a more normal distribution of importance scores.
The modal rating is 5, the median is 4, and the mean is 3.7.

Egos were asked to estimate the duration of each relationship
they had with an alter and their replies were coded into ten-
year strata (see Table 2). Most of the ego's relationships appear
to have lasted less than half the ego's lifetime. The mean duration for male egos is 35.8 years (S.D. 10.99) and 33.7 for females
(S.D. 13.67). The difference is not significant.

Persons interviewed reported about 40 percent of the network
alters are kin across the sample. While such a result is not surprising it is somewhat inconsistent with the "folk hypothesis"
that is frequently heard, that is, "we are all kin here." Both
network and ethnographic data indicate the importance of kinship.

A study that deals with a different mix of kin to nonkin is
We're All Kin:, A Cultural Study of a Mountain Neighborhood by F.
Carlene Bryant (1981). Bryant reports that in the mountain neighborhood she studied "all 198 residents are related, and that people make much of this in remarking upon their social world"

Table 2. Duration of Ego-Alter Relationships

0-9 years	16 percent
10-19 years	17 percent
20-29 years	15 percent
30-39 years	13 percent
40-49 years	14 percent
50-59 years	11 percent
60-69 years	10 percent
70-79 years	3 percent
80 and more	>1 percent
unspecified	1 percent

(1981:3). Bryant writes, "They are fond of explaining . . . that 'We're all at least a little bit kin,' that 'We're all one big happy family here'; and they stress this feature in comparing their neighborhood with American communities outside the mountains" (1981:3). Essentially similar statements are uttered by informants in Ridge County. In effect, their "everybody is related to everybody else" is an attempt to express the idea that large proportion of social relationships and interactions are between kin or affected by kinship. One can also argue that kinship serves as a kind of model for other kinds of relationships.

Kinship knowledge is used to track and interpret unfamiliar people. One expression of this strategy is the behavior one can observe when two people meet each other for the first time. I observed such a meeting during a visit to a nursing home in a nearby community with a church group from Ridge County. Kinship reckoning was part of the initial conversational framework. In talking with residents of the nursing home, visitors tried to identify the closest shared relative or perhaps an affiliation combining kinship links and other factors. Other kinds of affiliation might be churches or schools attended, neighborhoods lived in, and preachers baptized by. This discourse included references to places and experiences. As it unfolded, more individuals were drawn into the content of the discussion.

This phenomenon occurs in many contexts. Guest preachers at revivals may include kinship reckoning information about themselves in the opening remarks. I have observed discussions between political party election canvassers and prospective voters that included kinship reckoning information. The canvasser might, for example, present information about the candidate's kin in the community. While kinship is frequently used, people will also present reckoning information in the framework of school attendance, previous farm tenancies, neighboring relationships, as well as other kinds of relations. Although kin is important in these kinds of transactions it is necessary to emphasize that there is a more general process going on in these interchanges. In essence people are using existing relationships beyond the time and place of the current interaction to establish a new relationship. They are referencing themselves to the context rather than relying on the instrumentalities of the present interaction.

In the visit of the church group to the nursing home it is interesting to note that the process of reckoning applied only to those who were able to maintain a conversation and had sufficient memory to present kinship information of their own. It seems that a person who is not able to present kinship information showing who they are genealogically is less able to establish affiliation. It is likely that social isolation would increase in such a situation. Of course, in interpreting this example it is important to remember that much of the purpose of this activity is just to fill time in which there is not much "instrumental" going on.

Kin are clustered into large groups called families by community members. I was not able to estimate the portion of the community that was part of a family in this sense; certainly not everyone is. Some are part of family groups that are primarily focused somewhere else. Reckoning of these relationships is the focus of some avocational interest. There are numerous published and unpublished genealogies covering "families" in the study community. Some are regional in scope. The genealogies are usually published in hardcover, often in signed and numbered "collector's" editions. Other, less formal ones may only cover a few generations. Such documents are often supplemented with ubiquitous notes, letters, newspaper clippings, and newspaper obituaries stuffed in the family Bible or a shoebox. An individual can define a relationship with family groups on either the mother's or the father's side. Thus, surnames are not a reliable indicator of affiliation. In addition, people will recognize that they are related to a certain set of Joneses and not another. There is no apparent name for these different groups; when pressed, a person might say something like "That's a different batch of Wilsons" or "That's on the side of the Washington County Smiths." At bottom, people trace descent back to an early ancestor, usually a pioneer settler. Therefore, each family is linked to a place or region. Bryant uncovered a similar pattern and proposed a useful definition: "A family is thus composed of those kinfolk who are both genealogically and socially close and who invest their relationships to one another with cultural significance, tracing their descent and the social bonds believed to result from this to a common ancestor" (1981:53).

The linkage to place may be rendered through identification of a family "homeplace," perhaps the farmstead where the informant was raised. Some persons (probably a limited number) make a special effort to maintain ownership of the homeplace within the family. Sometimes the homeplace is the location of homecomings or family reunions, depending on their scale. If the homecoming simply involves children gathering to celebrate the birthday of their mother or father, the homeplace is a suitable site. Some reunions, however, are large regionwide events. For these, the local state park or the city park in the county seat is usually rented to accommodate the crowd. The activities may include a church service, a guest speaker, and almost always a "basket dinner." The primary activity is talk—recollection and comparison of the effects of time on the health and the size of the family.

Kin-group awareness extends beyond the members of the group into the community at large. That is, people, including nonmembers, are aware of who is in each group and who is outside. For example, there is a tendency to hold a person's kin responsible for helping in time of need. One informant said that anyone should help a person in need but noted that others thought such aid was the sole responsibility of kin. People also tend to evaluate others on the basis of family reputation. "You judge them," said one respondent, " by name. . . . You know just by the name, that's a reliable name and there's other names that's just kind of questionable. . . . [Some have] a reputation of being good, dependable, and upright. You can be friendly with everybody, but there're some people that you can't have that much in common with and you don't want your children to have that much in common with 'em."

Awareness of kin groupings is especially observable at estate sales. Frequently, in order to complete the probate process the possessions of an individual are sold. At these sales it is considered improper to bid against a relative of the deceased for real estate or other things. If a kinsman chooses to bid on an object, others will refrain from bidding. I have observed public apologies for breaches of this bit of etiquette at estate auctions. Of course, antiques dealers from outside the county do not know the relatives of the deceased, even if they are privy to the custom, and they often bid against relatives. For this reason, and because they often bid up prices, there seems to be a certain amount of hostility toward them. For the system to work, people must know who is related to other people. Prior to a sale the interests of family members will often be discussed within the community in order to ascertain whether the kin want to obtain what is being auctioned. Persons who are not kin sometimes buy objects at estate sales as a remembrance of the deceased. This kind of behavior applies to many county residents—less, of course, to new residents and more to families that have been in the county for a longer period of time.

Another aspect of kinship is the tendency for kinlike behaviors to be extended to friends and neighbors. Kinship is one model for effective human relationships. One woman, seated at the bedside of her dying husband, likened the support and concern she had received from members of the community to "having two thousand relatives." For her, supportive behavior was kinlike behavior. In other cases, kinship terms are extended. The practice occurs most frequently in the area of religious life. Most churches, especially the rural ones, follow the pattern of using kin terms among members. Many people think of fellow church members as "brothers and sisters in Christ," occasionally using kinship terms in contexts other than the church. The honorific applied to the preacher is also *brother*, and a few regard the Roman Catholic practice of calling the priest *father* as blasphemous, because it usurps a term for God for use in this world. The same few people would tend not to use the term *father* for their own father. Generally, the kin terms used are consistent with the alternatives reported by David M. Schneider for the American kinship system (1980). There is one alternative within the region and in Ridge County that is not identified in his admirably thorough analysis, however. The terms *mammaw* and *pappaw* are frequently heard, along with *grandma* and *grandpa* or the less frequent *mammy* and *pappy*.

The kin terms *uncle* and *aunt* may also be generally applied to certain community members. Interviews and old newspaper stories did not conclusively reveal the components of meaning associated with these terms, but certain attributes are common to those called aunt or uncle. The terms are used for long-term residents of advanced age, for whom the speaker feels affection and respect. Another element that may be associated with the use of these terms is dependence. In some cases, members of the community seemed to employ the terms for people they were encompassing in a kinlike caring relationship. In this context the social position of the uncle or aunt was as an appendage to an existing kin group. Ultimately, the term would come to be used by a wide array of people who were not party to the original relationship.

Like feelings about kin, feelings about neighbors are complex. Among the attributes of good neighbors was the provision of various kinds of practical support; yet the relationship is characterized by a certain reserve. As one person noted, "A good neighbor is interested in the things that affect you but still they are not intrusive." Relationships with neighbors may develop better if the ego and alter enter the relationship on equal terms. As another informant said, "If you're not envious of your neighbor, of what he has, there is no reason why you can't be a good neighbor." Another important aspect of this relationship is trust. Good relationships with neighbors are a source of pleasure, as one male noted. "If we don't have some feeling for our neighbors, then we aren't going to share and enjoy being with our neighbors or have the wholesome feelings that we have." Relationships between neighbors were often maintained for some time after the two moved apart.

Some very old informants noted that neighbors keep track of them during the day. As one eighty-three-year-old man said, "If they don't see me after a few hours, they come and check on me." This attention requires that he keep the neighbors informed about his whereabouts. One Sunday he forgot to tell his neighbors that he was going to church, and the neighbor ended up calling his son to find out if anything was wrong.

Neighbors frequently figure in the changing farming strategies of older people. They may help with livestock, usually under some type of economic arrangement. For example, neighbors who help may share in the calf crop or cut the hay on a share basis. The labor requirements for raising beef cattle are relatively low, but someone does need to be around.

Informants clearly discern a high level of neighborliness in the county, but they testify that there has been a reduction in the frequency and intensity of the these relationships. Some say that their neighbors are just too busy. Economic cooperation can be an important basis for a relationship with a neighbor, but there is less of this than in the past. This aspect of being a neighbor is also influenced by age. As an older male notes, "I worked with them when we was both younger and able to work. . . . But since he's grown older, I don't see him too much. Well, it's sad but I don't see too much of my neighbors."

In a sense, organization membership is unlike any other type of social organization, because it more clearly involves choice. Data collected on the entire population reveal a distribution of membership frequency across the ages from infant to elderly that is best described as a whale-backed curve. There is a peak in voluntary association membership in the high school years, followed by a precipitous drop during the early twenties. This valley is followed by cohort-by-cohort increases until a new peak appears at the 65-69 category. When voluntary association and church affiliation are combined, the peak level of social involvement is the 65-69 age category, which is marked by the highest level of church affiliation of any age category (84 percent) and a relatively high level of voluntary association membership. In the age category 80 and over, both church affiliation and voluntary association membership is somewhat lower. There is little comparable data in the literature on voluntary association membership through the entire life-span. Data reported by Selz C. Mayo on a measure of social participation in voluntary associations through the entire age span of a rural North Carolina population showed a very similar whale-back distribution (Mayo 1950).

Older men and women tend to belong to certain kinds of organizations. Among older males there is a greater tendency to belong to secret lodges and veterans groups. Older women have often been members of homemakers clubs for a long time. In addition to these secular organizations churches sponsor club-like groups for persons of different age groups. Voluntary associations of all these types will often send get-well cards to their members, frequently crossing denominational boundaries. Age-related church groups other than Sunday school classes are much more frequent in town churches. This seems to be a function of the way that the minister is hired. Most town churches have larger budgets and full-time, professionally trained preachers, but because small churches are considered entry-level positions in a preaching career, these ministers are often quite young. They tend to bring with them "innovative" programs, in some cases special programs for older people. The most elaborate of such programs involved taking overnight trips within the region and paying for a bus and motel. Participants expressed how much they enjoyed these outings. The same church also had a "tape ministry" for shut-ins.

Preachers and other persons interested in the growth or maintenance of their churches membership need to carefully attend to issues of age-specific programming. A frequently cited problem older people have in conjunction with church attendance is the discomfort caused by the hard pews and loss of body fat padding as they age. People also speak of "warm" and "cold" churches. Many people would agree that the country churches tend to be warmer, that is, more friendly and providing more interaction. One preacher felt that churches grew by being attractive to adults with young children. He felt that this type of congregation member desired growth and improvement in the church, whereas older members were satisfied with stability if it was associated with warm affect. In his commitment to growth, he worked to improve the physical facilities of the church with air conditioning and new pews and carpet. His wife led a young adults group. Other churches used a strategy based on attracting children.

The now-small category of co-workers has little impact on present networks, but increased industrialization will certainly change this pattern. People from the county commute together, and the typical half-hour trip provides them with the opportunity to get to know each other well. In addition, those employed in industry often act as brokers of information about jobs.

The largest number of alters are classified as friends, and the wide application of this category supports the view that friendship is generalized as nearly any kind of positive relationship. In contrast to Claude S. Fischer's analysis, in Ridge County *friend* does not mean close non-kin (1982). Obviously most kin are also regarded as friends, and they were also so regarded historically. Farm-raised informants report that when they were young all or most of their friends were kin. Clearly the treatment of kin and friend as discrete categories in communities like Ridge County is inappropriate if local meanings are respected. Of best friends, at least some are confidants, people to whom, as one informant stated you can say, "all your words," for whom you have "utter trust."

Fischer presents a very useful discussion of social research focused on friendship. He makes the point that though research on friendship is burgeoning, conceptualization is undeveloped and problematic. In Fischer's words, "An important difficulty with this promising literature is that much of the research is built on a weak foundation: the concept of 'friend.' Theoretical discussions typically use the term in a taken-for-granted manner; research studies ask people about friends as if that concept were obvious. 'Friend', however, is actually very ambiguous. Its ambiguity creates problems in trying to interpret reports of friendships and therefore in trying to explain it or to use it as an indicator of social involvement" (1982:287-88). Despite these problems, Fischer believes research on friendship should not be abandoned, for "it is too important a 'folk concept,' an idea that people use to order their worlds" (1982:288). One promising approach is to collect social data as I have done here, in terms of the more concrete notion of social interaction rather than culturally fuzzy concepts like friendship. This approach can be combined with a commitment to preserve the meanings extant in the community by taking a cognitive or ethnosemantic perspective (Pike 1954), by doing general ethnography as in this project, or a domain analysis. A good model for such an analysis is the work of Gloria J. Wentkowski (1981).

5. The Networks

They had been married sixty-two years. Over a year ago Paul had resigned as head usher at church after what the doctor in Aberdeen had described as a little stroke. It happened on a terribly hot Friday afternoon in August. He was trying to cut the grass before the weekend. Most people tried to clean up their yards late Fridays or Saturday if they had a job in town. He felt all right now, but he tired out more quickly and had to work harder at keeping track of things. Nettie, well Nettie was the same old Nettie, she'd speak her mind and cut through pretense.

Nettie's problems started with a ladder. She was in the loft of the barn on Friday cleaning out some old junk. Deciding to go back to the house to rest, she started slowly backing down the ladder she had used to get to the loft. The ladder, she said, just started "wavering" and fell over. She called out for Paul. Deciding he needed to get her into the house, Paul rigged up a cart from an old lawn mower bottom that he used to haul dirt and fertilizer around his garden. Once they were inside she told him to call Sarah, their daughter-in-law, who soon rushed over, along with Nettie's two sons. They called the doctor, who had them call Mr. Wilson, who ran the ambulance service. Nettie and Paul knew Mr. Wilson well, and they also knew his father, his brother, his wife and children. When he arrived, he speculated that the leg was broken. Nettie, flat on her back in the Chevy station wagon that served as an ambulance, rode the forty-five miles to the city hospital.

That afternoon the minister called to find out what had happened and where they took Nettie. It was not clear how he had heard about the fall. Sunday morning he'd say something about it at church. The first to send a card was Nettie's Bible school class. Many of the group had recently traveled to the Smoky Mountains with Paul and Nettie and the rest of the Golden Agers Club from the church. It was some days before Paul was able to arrange for a ride to the hospital to see her.

Even though they had been married for such a long time and really loved each other, they would still argue. The main issue was why the ladder fell. Finally, as he was leaving, she raised the question about whether they should sell the house. She was characteristically insistent that they had to move out before winter. Their son, in an earlier visit, had told them that they ought to sell off their property and move in with him. To her it seemed a bad choice; moving in, even with family, would be hard. As she put it, if she came to "live on someone else's stuff," she'd get bossed around. Anybody who knew Nettie knew that she did not take to getting bossed around.

The accident forced Nettie and Paul to consider making some changes, the kind of changes that had probably been anticipated, if not concretely planned. For us, the incident illustrates the great utility embedded in a person's social network. Here, where I will consider social relationships in rather abstract terms, their experience illustrates the concrete substance of networks and how useful they are for dealing with circumstances.

This component of the analysis addresses a fundamental question in social gerontology, "What are the differences in social life of older people of different ages?" To answer the question it is necessary to view it from both morphological and interaction perspectives. Especially important is the relationship between age and network size because of the implications for social gerontology theory. Also important are differences in the composition and structure of the networks of men and women and some individual and community factors that shape networks.

Network size is taken to be the number of alters reported in the interview. In these interviews respondents reported networks ranging from 3 to 105 persons, a considerable variation. Mean network size was 24.9. The standard deviation was 16.35. The median was 21, indicating the influence of the scattering of very large networks. The intertercile range was 18 to 26.

The relationship between age and network size is an important dimension of the analysis because it complements social

Table 3. Mean Network Size By Age Group

64 and below	23.8
65 to 69	31.2
70 to 74	29.0
75 to 79	21.4
80 and above	19.0

Note: F value = 2.91. DF = (4,134). Significant at the .025 level. The differences between the means of the five categories were examined using the ONEWAY anova procedure in MINITAB release 5.1.3.

gerontological research done in response to the theories of social engagement. There is little reported research on age differences in social networks. Only one of the studies I have chosen for comparison reports any data on such differences in networks. In the original formulation of the research problem a simple negative linear relationship between network size and age was posited. That is, I expected persons in older age strata to have smaller networks. In a sense, the data supported this hypothesis (see Table 3), but the addition of the younger age stratum makes the network size distribution curvilinear.[1]

That is to say, aging brings the growth of social networks and then the decline anticipated in the literature. The so-called young-old strata; 65-69 and 70-75, show mean network size larger than the sample mean. Compared to the youngest stratum (60 to 64), network size increases markedly in the 65 to 69 age stratum. This stratum is the peak, following which there is a gradual decline in size of networks. The networks of those 80 and above have the smallest mean size, but it is only slightly smaller than that of the 75 to 79 stratum. Further, the networks of these two strata are closer in size to that of the youngest age group, than to those of the 65 to 69 and 70 to 74 strata. It is apparent that the pattern of development of social networks with age is complex. There are statistically significant differences be-

1. This distribution shows the importance of observing the entire life-span when processes of social aging are researched, and is indicative of some of the distortions in understanding that can be created by research that is limited strictly to the older age cohorts.

tween age strata; the largest between adjacent strata is the increase in network size between the group of those 64 or younger
and that aged 65 to 69. This increase in mean network size is
7.3, or 23 percent. Between the peak stratum, 65 to 69, and the
lowest, 80 and over, there is a decrease of 12.2 alters, or 39
percent. Clearly the inclusion of the youngest age stratum
changes the meaning of the linear pattern of decline in social
involvement frequently observed and explained in the context
of social gerontological research. Had the same sample been
drawn with people sixty-five years old and older, rather than
sixty and older, the results would have been unambiguously
linear and negative. The data presented in Table 3 make it necessary to ask if the late-life decline in social involvement is simply
a return to mid-life levels from a period of postretirement social
elaboration.

Discussions of social involvement do not usually consider
how much is enough or what the limits are. There has been at
least one attempt to "norm" the idea of social networks. Based
on data collected on the networks of two hundred psychologically normal, urban individuals, psychiatrist E. Mansell Pattison
and his colleagues suggest that "the normal person has a finite
primary group of about 25 people" (1975:1249). Working from
a theoretical model based on human information-processing
limitations (Miller 1956) Peter Killworth and H. Russell Bernard
posited a range of 24 to 27 persons as normal (1974). Recognizing
the somewhat speculative nature of these conclusions, we can
claim that the network size of 25 represents a kind of comparative
standard.

Graph theory, a kind of mathematics which allows simulation
of important social network properties, suggests additional relevant network properties in reference to size. Perhaps most important is the effect of network size on what graph theorists call
matrix distance, expressed simply as the number of links it takes
to go from one node to another in a graph. If a community of
persons is viewed in matrix terms as a set of potentially linked
nodes, and network size is the number of links from one node
to other nodes, it becomes clear that distance to all other nodes
declines if network size is higher. The linkage routes are shorter.
As the network size approaches N-1, matrix distance approaches
the minimum 1. The variable of reachability is a sociological

expression of this property (Doreian 1974). Reaching someone through someone else is common and important in Ridge County, as it is in almost any community. While this aspect is usually thought of in instrumental terms, there is a purely cognitive dimension that is also important. When a person is reachable through another person it is likely that the two persons will share knowledge of each other, a fundamental aspect of social solidarity.

Graph theory associated with matrices is useful for demonstrating the underlying structural properties of these sets of linked nodes, including the fact that a linkage from one person to another will decrease distance to nodes beyond the nodes directly linked to the person. Reality forms a very fuzzy version of the structural properties demonstrated by graph theory, and concomitantly, the clean and unambiguous properties of a graph theory matrix mask the complexities of everyday life. Nevertheless, they tell us much that is important. Perhaps the most important point is that the difference between a network of 25 and 24 may be trivial but it is not simply 1. This relates to one component of Killworth and Bernard's theoretical optimum discussed above, the "small world" phenomenon. That is, beginning with any individual who is connected, it is possible to extend the relationships beyond the persons that individual has ties with. Rather soon it will be demonstrated that the individual is linked to everybody in the country (Berkowitz 1982:16). This is not to make the point that everybody in the Ridge County sample is within steps of contact with the president of the United States, but something that is really very important. If an ego, such as a member of the sample, is linked to more people, then contact with anyone can be made more rapidly and more people potentially know about ego. The foundation of concern is knowledge.

The pattern of composition of networks varies with network size in a number of ways. This analysis was done by grouping networks into three size categories by dividing the total frequency distribution into thirds. The small network group comprised networks of up to 18 alters, medium network group included networks 19 to 25 alters, and the large network group contained those of at least 26 alters. These categories were examined using the X^2 test.

Table 4. Kinship Status of Alters by Network Size

	Nonkin		Kin		
	Actual	Expected	Actual	Expected	Total
Small network group	295	(348)	289	(236)	584
Medium network group	587	(629)	464	(425)	1,051
Large network group	1,186	(1,094)	649	(741)	1,835
Total	2,068		1,402		3,470

Note: X^2 = 45.454; DF = 2; Prob = 0.0001.

I analyzed the network alter classifications—kin, neighbors, co-workers, fellow organization members, and friend—to determine their relationship to network size. The analysis revealed that as network size increased the percentage of kin decreased in a statistically significant way. Across the sample, just over 40 percent of the alters were classified as kin by the egos, but large networks are formed from nonkin. The values in Table 4 are the observed number of alters in the networks of the three size strata and the expected number of alters. In small networks, alters that are kin are 122 percent of the expected. For large networks kin are 87 percent of the expected.

In contrast to the kinship category of alters, there was no significant difference in the neighbor category among the network size groups. In large networks somewhat fewer persons are classified as neighbors than in other categories, as one would expect, but overall, the neighbor category is relatively constant across the categories (X^2 = 2.711; DF = 2; Prob = 0.2578). The co-worker category, however, contributed relatively more to the composition of the largest network, than to the medium and small networks (X^2 = 26.528, DF = 2, Prob = 0.0001). Of course, the absolute number of co-workers in the sample is small. The co-worker pattern also applies to fellow members of organizations. The largest network size group includes a relatively greater number of fellow organization members than do the small and medium network size group (X^2 = 64.386; DF = 2; Prob = 0.0001). The alters categorized as friends are relatively less frequent in the largest network size category than they are in the small and medium categories. The pattern is similar to that exhibited for the kin category (X^2 = 56.106; DF = 2; Prob = 0.0001).

To review, kin and friends contribute relatively less to the large networks, but all networks contain similar proportions of neighbors. Co-workers and fellow organization members appear relatively more frequently in the networks categorized as large. It is possible that large networks are "achieved" through affiliation with organizations beyond the kin group and friendship; that is, in part, by participation in more formal social structures. This pattern may be consistent with the idea of a core network of more complex and perhaps more intimate relationships, supplemented in the case of some individuals with less complex and perhaps less intimate relationships. Network growth could occur through the addition of substantially different kinds of individual relationships, but verification of this view would require longitudinal data.

Examination of network alters who are kin revealed another noteworthy characteristic. Analysis of the numbers of males and females showed that kinship network alters tended to be female, a finding anticipated in the literature (X^2 = 7.028; DF = 1; Prob. = 0.008).

Analysis of the frequency of interaction in relationships and network size shows significant differences between the small, medium, and large networks. The X^2 test demonstrated that the large networks contain a relatively large number of low-frequency encounters. The small and medium networks had relatively greater numbers of high-frequency relationships. In small networks 22.3 percent of the links were activated every day, whereas in large networks only 12.5 percent were of that frequency category. Distance may not be as important a factor as one would imagine. Some maintain quite frequent contacts at great distance via telephone. The daughter of one woman called her about three times a week from Tennessee.

I examined network size in terms of the variables in the general category of communication resources: car ownership, possession of a driver's license, having a telephone, and the presence of a self-reported physical impairment. I assumed that these variables would be positively associated with larger networks, but only one followed the predicted pattern, and that relationship was very weak. There were no differences in network size between those with a driver's license and those without on the basis of the X^2 test (X^2 = 1.071; DF = 2; Prob = 0.5853). The analysis of car ownership produced similar results. People who owned cars were not more likely to appear in the large network group (X^2 = 2.439; DF = 2; Prob. = 0.2988). Nor was telephone availability related to network size (X^2 = 2.728; DF = 2; Prob. = 0.2556). The analysis of self-reported impairment and network size revealed a marginal association in the predicted direction (X^2 = 4.627; DF = 2; Prob. = 0.0989).

The data on the duration of relationships was used to group them into three broad categories: short duration (0 to 19 years), medium duration (20 to 39 years), and long duration (40 and more years). About a third of ego-alter relationships are in the short-duration category. The medium-duration category includes just under 28 percent of the relationships. The long-duration category has more relationships in it than any other category, just under 40 percent. These categories were examined in terms of their relationship with the three network size strata (see Table 5). Large social networks have relatively fewer long-duration relationships. Small networks have a higher frequency of them. Over 45 percent of the relationships in small networks are forty years or longer in duration, whereas 35 percent of the relationships in the large network group are of that duration. As a corollary, 28 percent of the relationships in small networks are of short duration, compared to 36 percent of those in large networks.

Longer-term relationships display a number of expected features. First, these relationships tend to based on kinship. In the long-duration category the kin and nonkin alters each make up 50 percent. In the short-duration category the nonkin alters make up 69.5 percent. The medium-duration category percentages are very close to the general pattern of 60 percent nonkin and 40 percent kin (X^2 = 91.092; DF = 2; Prob. = 0.0001).

Better understanding of the complex relationships between choice and social interaction awaits studies specifically focused on choice, rather than the outcome of choice. Here, I will consider data relating to choices people make about social participation—whether or not to participate. Further, I will consider the issue of choice from the standpoint of the community, for

Table 5. Relationship Duration by Network Size

	Small Network Group	Medium Network Group	Large Network Group	Percentage of all Networks
Short duration				
Actual	163	310	663	33
Expected	(191)	(344)	(600)	
Medium duration				
Actual	156	292	520	28
Expected	(163)	(293)	(512)	
Long duration				
Actual	265	450	653	39
Expected	(230)	(414)	(723)	
Percentage of all networks	17	30	53	

Note: X^2 = 29,587; DF = 4; Prob = 0.0001.

the observable social organization of a community is a product of individual and group decisions to interact or not, based on generalized principles as well as specific circumstances. Most of the network analysis is directed at understanding the outcomes of individual choice to interact.

In Ridge County, as in many other communities, there are people who never leave the house. Reclusivity is infrequently mentioned in the literature on social aging, and certainly it is a rare phenomenon in Ridge County. Of course, people of any age can be confined by sickness or invalidism, but there are others who simply do not go out. This behavior may be temporary; for example, someone who has failed to meet an obligation may deal with the failure by assuming aspects of the sick role. In cases we observed, the person who adopted this role provided an ostensible medical explanation. One person became reclusive because of an approaching social obligation that made this person most uncomfortable. The isolation lasted about six months. It can be permanent, however. Sometimes, people simply decide they would rather not go out.

In Ridge County people whose physical condition prevents

them from going out are called shut-ins, and the term implies rather lengthy involuntary immobility. Members of the community attend to shut-ins in a number of ways. Most church congregations pray for them as a collective category and also individually. Almost every church practices visitation, either by the preacher or by the lay leaders of the church. There may be an effort to serve communion to shut-in members, for some churches hold it necessary for the believer to have communion every Sunday. In the town churches with professional clergy the visitation is done largely by the preacher. One preacher at a town church made regular visits to six shut-in members of the "church family." The visits did not have any ritual content and consisted mostly of friendly conversation, which the preacher happened to be very good at. About the visits he said, "During the winter especially they are confined to their room and they just need someone to talk to. You may go for ten minutes and just not say anything. I believe this is something older people need and feel." Church members in nursing homes are also visited.

When people get sick and seek care, network links are activated. For the most part, primary health care is provided by physicians outside the county. If the health problem is more significant individuals may be admitted to hospitals in adjacent counties or perhaps in Lexington. Some select the hospital because it is more accessible to potential visitors. It is apparent that people are able to track the "acute" care system, as is especially important at the secondary and tertiary levels of health care. People from certain parts of the county tend to go to certain predictable locations, and so the alter has the knowledge necessary to visit or send a get-well card. I visited a number of people in the hospital and found that some individuals would receive only a few cards from their children but others would receive hundreds. Those who received many cards were sure to comment on their numbers.

In a sense these visitations and communications occurred along "routes" or "channels" that were familiar to community members because they would have visited hospitalized people or shopped in these locations frequently in the past. Chronic care facilities are resorted to in a less familiar sequence than acute care facilities. Thus, someone who is shunted from an acute care facility to a chronic care facility during the course of treatment can be temporarily lost to the alters. I have observed situations where a spouse had trouble locating the hospitalized person, and the uncertainty, however momentary, put great stress on this important relationship. The ironic contrast between the bureaucratic description of the structure of the care system and the fear of loss of a loved one is noteworthy. The system works, but only with a kind of turbulence.

In such circumstances alters cooperated to find the ego. One might refer to this behavior, which relates to the idea of reachability, as "tracking" or simply as maintaining knowledge of location so a person can be reached. Churches functioned well as clearinghouses for this information because they are regular meeting places and make public announcements of the condition of individuals.

Although all churches perform this function, the congregations of rural churches spend much more time in informal conversation before and after the service. "After church," said one informant, "they'll walk out and stand there and visit . . . Maybe you won't see 'em all . . . but at different times you'll see 'em and talk to 'em. And in summer when it's pretty, many times people go early, well say twenty or thirty minutes before church." Male interaction often involves substantial amounts of discussion relating to farming activities. Perhaps most noteworthy are discussions about unfamiliar technology, weather and rainfall, plans to cooperate on an activity, and potential transactions.

One could argue that the older person who values contact benefits from regular and predictable interaction because it allows their network alters to "track" them and facilitates communication. Churches and other voluntary associations enhance the ability of members to "track" other members, but only those who attend regularly. If a person's attendance is erratic, absence does not generate concern; erratic attendance does not provide a reliable communication channel. I have observed cases in which people who attended church "every time the doors were open" were absent. The members evaluated the absence as a sign of crisis that had to be attended to immediately.

In churches information on members in hospitals and nursing homes is presented in what are called prayer lists. Usually an elder has the responsibility to put together a list of those who are sick. He seeks out information on people within the church, friends and relatives of church members, and prominent members of the community. These names are read, and then a prayer is offered. The list is also included in church bulletins and newsletters, which apparently are mailed to anyone who requests them. Newsletters of one church often go to members of other churches, and word of illness or other misfortune spreads widely throughout the churched community. Persons who respond to the information by visiting receive diffuse rewards for being a "good Christian" or for investing time in "Christian witness." The rewards for the here and now take the form of respect and also reciprocity with members of the church, who respond in a like manner when the person has a similar need. Ostensibly prayer lists and prayer are intended to "call forth the healing power of God if it be His will" through the "Body of Christ," or the church, but the latent function is to make available health status and locational information about community members in a way that makes the information more motivating for many. The information creates a web of symbolically based relationships.

One theme in Ridge County preaching, to be taken up a bit later, is the potential immortality of social networks. Those who are saved will be able to maintain their relationships with other Christians "on the other side." In this world, too, aspects of the network continue after the death of the ego. The funeral brings people from far away together again. Indeed, it may be the most effective institution of all for uniting dispersed people. Said one informant, "The thing that brings more people back to the county than anything else are funerals. People know that they are going to see other people that they haven't seen for many, many years." In death as in life network alters supply food for the gathering.

Some people are buried in family burying grounds, but the most frequently used cemeteries are associated with churches and held by cemetery companies in which stock is issued. Members of the network of the deceased return to visit the grave, mostly on Memorial Day Sunday. At a large church-related cemetery visitors may be asked during this time to contribute to the maintenance fund, which provides for lawn mowing and other activities. About a third of the contributions come from

Ridge County. The rest come from other Kentucky counties and a few from other states. Some families are still linked with the dead after many years. It is interesting to see how the visitors after a while lose acquaintance with the persons who remained in the community. As time passes the relationship with local cemetery administrators becomes more and more anonymous.

Church visitation demonstrates an aspect of the operations of social organization—that social behavior is a product of choice, but the choice of the alters as well as the ego. Those being visited are expected to behave in a certain way, to express appreciation for the visit, for example. The social life of the churches illustrates different aspects of this phenomenon. In addition to visitation, there are many examples of group decisions that structure the social interactions of church members. The decisions may be made by the preacher, Sunday school director, or elders. Visitation represents a decision to maintain contact with an individual. In addition, church people will make decisions about the age structure of the Sunday school classes, which tends to separate younger from older church members. Age limits may be combined with rules about marital status. For example, in a town church one class was structured by a policy that the total age of married couples could not be more than seventy. When the age exceeded seventy, the couple had to go on to the next class.

There is no widely used term for people who are perceived as being able to go out but who do not. The role is not as highly conceptualized as is the shut-in role. These people may be called recluses, but they are not shut-ins because they have, in the interpretation of the community, "decided" to stay in. In other words, the difference between a shut-in and a recluse is community understanding of the basis of the person's decision making. Most of those identified as recluses are women. One informant asserted that "it was always a woman, you know, that was a recluse." The same person suggested that there had been recluses in town all her life, though, as she said, "I never saw them during their lifetime." In the course of collecting network data at least one recluse was interviewed.

This person has an active social network, which, though about half the average size, is in many ways technically indistinguishable from those of nonreclusive persons. The chief difference is that most of her interaction takes place either in her own living room when friends and relatives call, over the telephone, or through intermediaries. A preteen neighborhood girl drops in during the day to run errands. A young nephew goes to get the mail and groceries. This recluse does go out occasionally but not routinely or as a positively valued experience. Her reclusive behavior started with the death of her husband. The point is that a network can be well developed even when a person decides to stay home. Members of the community may continue to try to get the person involved. This woman has been invited to visit the Senior Citizens Center but did not go, she said, because she was "not a good mixer" and she liked her own cooking. In one case a friend encouraged her to come back to church. She answered, "I've got three good preachers on TV every Sunday. I am not going to go there where you people are fighting all the time." This remark suggests something of the dynamics of reclusivity. It seems that recluses find it painful to go out; and they feel that they will be subjected to what they regard as continual low-level criticism and bickering.

Reclusiveness is one form of avoidance, another aspect of individual choices. In social anthropology avoidance refers to the institutionalized inhibition of social interaction between persons of specific relationship. I use the term in a more generalized sense to refer to a person's choice not to speak with or socialize with other individuals. In network analysis, of course, data are collected from those who have made the antithetical choice; that is, informants choose to speak. Thus, avoidance is not very apparent in the flow of interaction that is social organization, but it is there, and perhaps it is more apparent in dense communities such as Ridge County. Sending someone else to the store, for example, might be a way of avoiding the storekeeper after an argument, or someone might communicate with an estranged parent through a grandchild. Sometimes the avoided person will attempt to reach the ego through another person with whom ego is still speaking. In other words, communication may still occur. Such "antirelations" can develop in spite of kinship and long-term association. They are often the product of a "falling-out" associated with an argument or assumed moral trespass. Churchgoers are encouraged to avoid some general categories of people. Mainstream preachers might express the idea that a

Christian should not associate with non-Christians, except in the world of business and in attempts to convert them. At the same time, Christians are exhorted to associate with other Christians by regularly attending church. This theme seems to be more frequently expressed in Holiness churches.

Churches and other community groups can make decisions that will change aspects of a person's formal involvement in the organization—for example, voting someone out of a leadership position, although this is reported as rare. Older Sunday school teachers are sometimes removed because those in their classes can no longer understand them. Great bitterness can result in such cases, and the teacher's kin may even limit church attendance. More typically, the person sees trouble coming and steps aside. Some churches have an informal concept of the *elder emeritus*, allowing older people to retain the title but not giving them any major responsibility. As one woman expressed it, older people were "still officers and still leaders but someone else was actually doing the work." Some churches have a corollary policy of drawing younger members, especially males, into leadership positions so they can develop. Under this strategy, males in their late teens are introduced to the simpler aspects of ritual in anticipation of later service as deacon or elder.

Another community influence on the social interaction of older people is the federally supported Senior Citizens Center, located in the county seat. The center serves regular group lunches, arranges for house weatherization, and runs the "Meals on Wheels" program, as well as other programs. The community chose to take advantage of available subsidies to establish the program; program managers choose to build a clientele through "outreach;" and older people choose to participate or not. Program personnel put together an attractive and well-attended program with limited resources.

I considered participation in the program from a variety of perspectives.[2] Participation tended to be highest among town-dwelling females, but there was no relationship between participation and educational attainment, labor force participation,

2. Participation was evaluated by comparing the characteristics of the program participants to those of the general population using X^2. The data were obtained in a countywide census survey.

church attendance, voluntary association membership, or place of birth. Overall participation is 11 percent of the population age sixty and over, which is within the range of participation reported by other studies (Harris 1978; Schneider, Danforth, and Voth, 1980; Downing 1957; Powers and Bultena 1974). Only 17 percent of the participants are males. It is not unusual for male participation to be low. In a study of senior center participation in a number of upstate New York communities, P. Taietz found male participation rates of 25 percent (1976), as did R. Storey in an early study of a center in a northern California city (1962). In a more recent study of a center in the rural South, Ann W. Yearwood and Paula L. Dressel note, "As appears customary in such sites, females far outnumber males in attendance" (1983:513).

It is safe to conclude that these programs are generally less attractive to males than to females, but none of these studies seeks to explain why. In Ridge County older men do get together to talk, but they do it in "unsponsored" circumstances, congregating in smaller groups at various times during the day. Philip Drucker, who often joined these informal gatherings, said they had a "men's house" ambience, likening them to the male societies found in Micronesia, where he has done extensive work. The size of a group would change during the day, as men came and went. Women have much more precedent for gathering with other women at specific times and places during the week for conversation, food, and some kind of program. Homemakers clubs and church groups follow this pattern of activity, and so does the Senior Center, albeit on a larger scale. There is no similar precedent for males.

There are two dominant reasons given for not participating in the program. Some regard it as a type of welfare, for which they do not see a need. As one informant noted, "People are spoiled these days by this giveaway stuff." This view of the program, almost always expressed by males, was enhanced by the income-eligibility criterion for participation in certain programs administered by center staff. In the early days of the center, the staff stressed that the program was a service older people had earned, and as taxpayers all their lives, they were entitled to it. Local leaders strenuously worked to avoid any kind of eligibility requirements that might convey the idea of poverty.

Some people had no qualms about the stigma of welfare but chose not to participate anyway. Older women commented that the programs were uninteresting and that participation involved dealing with much petty gossip. For many others, however, the programs represented very pleasant opportunities to come together with friends.

The sex of the ego has much import for social life in Ridge County. For the most part people perceive men and women as quite different social entities, and there is only limited interchangeability in social roles. This way of constructing society is changing. Ridge Countians testify that the extent of male-female role segregation has declined, just as they say that people are not as independent and self-reliant as they used to be. Substantial cohort effect across the age span of the entire population is implied. Indeed, the strength of sex-role segregation varies in terms of generation. Older people make a sharp demarcation between roles; younger people seem to be more flexible. Paradoxically, the older people, who value independence and individual self-determination and who lament their demise, also consider women to be somehow dependent on men.

People agreed that men and women had different kinds of problems in aging. Some think men have more difficulty. For one reason, less of the socially acceptable work of men can be carried into later life, because it is heavier. Women are able to continue to practice what younger people might think of as hobbies: sewing, stitchery, and quilting. These were essential kinds of production, however, in the semisubsistence households in which these women were raised. In Ridge County when these persons were young, there was relatively little male craft activity, but females were involved in richly expressive craft production.

The social networks of male and female Ridge Countians manifest both similarities and differences. The sizes of networks are virtually identical; both men and women average about 25. Men and women vary in terms of their capacity to get around and be with others (see Table 1). For example, men are more likely to own cars and have driver's licenses. Presumably as a kind of compensation, women have a greater percentage of phones. A somewhat greater percentage of males than females reported impairments that would limit their mobility, but the difference is not significant statistically.

Slightly over 35 percent of the alters were a different sex from the egos, and these relationships were evenly divided between male and female egos. The ratios of same-sex alters to cross-sex alters are relatively stable across the age strata. The relationships between co-workers, fellow members of organizations, friends and neighbors tended to be between persons of the same sex. A comparison across the sample of ego's age and the sexual composition of the link revealed a substantial increase in the number of female-female relationships later in life, paralleled by a decrease in the relative number of male-male relationships.

Male-male relationships comprised fewer kinship relationships than other kinds; 73 percent of the male-male relationships were with nonkin. The female-female relationships were 60 percent nonkin, exactly the same as the samplewide pattern. Cross-sex relationships generally tend to be between kin. Same-sex co-worker relationships are more common than cross-sex ones for both male and female egos. Both male and female same-sex relationships were of greater frequency than expected ($X^2 = 23.216$; DF = 3; Prob. = 0.0001). Male egos have very few relationships with females classified as co-workers, only 0.4 percent of all alters. The most common co-worker relationship was between females, 2.45 percent of all alters and 42 percent of all co-worker ego-alter relationships. The male-male co-worker relationship appeared in 2.16 percent of all alters and 37 percent of all co-workers. The relationship with alters classified as fellow members of organizations revealed a different pattern. There were more than the expected number of such relationships between females and less than the expected number between all other combinations of egos and alters ($X^2 = 121.480$; DF = 3; Prob. = 0.0001). Of all such relationships 52 percent were between females, slightly more than twice as many as between males. The male and female cross-sex relationships in this category were about equal, 11 percent for male egos and female alters and 12 percent for female egos and male alters. This difference in the relationship between association membership, the sex of the ego, and ego's network is a function of the types of organizations available for males and females. The relationship between neighbors is a mirror image of the relationship between organization members. Its frequency was greater than expected between males and less than expected in the other three combinations (X^2 = 47.352; DF = 3; Prob. = 0.0001). The cross-sex relationships are essentially equal. "Best friends" tend to be of the same sex as the ego, whether male or female, and both male-male and female-female best-friend relationships are more numerous than expected (X^2 = 6.286; DF = 3; Prob. = 0.0946). Female-female relationships are 42 percent of all the best-friend relationships. The cross-sex relationship categories in this framework are essentially equal, each accounting for just over 13 percent of the best friend category. About 30 percent are male-male.

As Ridge County theology would suggest, the mean duration of social networks "in the world" of slightly more than thirty years is trivial. What we are calling network linkages have the potential to last an eternity, for those who are saved through confession and baptism will be reunited with kin after death. Virtually all church services conclude with an invitation to the unsaved to "walk down the aisle" and give the "good confession." As enticement, they are reminded that families will be reunited "on the other side." In a typical sermon preached one Memorial Day or Decoration Day (as it is sometimes called in Ridge County) one preacher addressed his congregation:

My friends today, ladies and gentlemen, boys and girls, moms and dads, have you prepared your life? Have you prepared your life for eternity? Are you ready to meet Jesus if Jesus would come today? I know today that there is a lot of people thinking [about kin] because you have lost your loved ones. And this is around the time, what we call Memorial Day, and we'd remember. We'd remember them very vividly in our minds, and there is a lot of sadness. But the thing of it is, have you prepared to meet mom and dad? Have you prepared to meet your wife, your husband? Have you made these preparations?

Age is related to salvation in only one way: all the churches agree that each person must make an individual choice for Christ. Therefore they unanimously practice adult baptism, which is consistent with the Anabaptist tradition in Protestant history. Only the Methodists will sometimes baptize infants, and then only rarely. For purposes of baptism, "adults" can be as young as ten years old. The ceremony is preceded by no formal training, although preachers will attempt to make sure that the young person is making an informed and sincere decision. When those being baptized are especially young, the preacher may comment on the informed and sincere nature of their decision. The idea that it does not matter at what age a person makes a "decision for Christ" is quite well developed, although some may note that it is better to be saved early so there will be time to "repay God for His sacrifice." Apostle Paul is cited as an example of a person who "came to Christ late in life." Most believe that an older person who was not physically able to baptized but who "confessed Christ" would be saved by intent. The waters of baptism are viewed as emblematic, and the act is one of obedience. While people may speak of themselves as "new Christians" with the need to spiritually develop, this state follows salvation. It is not a cause of salvation. The only requirements are a sincere declaration of faith and baptism. A life of accumulated sin is irrelevant to salvation. Human beings are saved through grace.

The relationship between males and females is driven and manifested by both a material and symbolic order.[3] The material order is the pattern of economic organization of the agrarian household, which characterized this community and probably most other frontier settlements. The symbolic order is the Genesis myth, interpreted as a statement that women are derived from men and dependent on them.

"And the Lord God said, It is not good that the man should be alone, I will make him an help meet for him. . . . And the Lord God caused a deep sleep to fall upon Adam, and he slept; and he took one of his ribs, and closed up the flesh instead

3. The idea of order resembles concepts like key symbol (Ortner 1973) and refers to fundamental systems of arrangement. Both the material and symbolic order should be thought of as both cause and effect. It is apparent, however, that material factors have primacy in processes of historical change and that the symbolic order has primacy in social discourse about the relationships. It is useful to think of social reality as an image reflected from two mirrors that face and reflect each other. These mirrors represent the material and symbolic arrangements that are in place. The images that they reflect include the reality presented in life.

thereof. And the rib, which the Lord God had taken from man, he made into a woman, and brought her unto the man. And Adam said, This is now bone of my bones, and flesh of my flesh; she shall be called Woman, because she was taken out of Man" (Gen.2). Sherry B. Ortner speaks of key symbols (1973) as culturally important, psychologically powerful, pervasive, culturally elaborated, and associated with restrictions. This part of Scripture can by analogy be thought of as a key text. That is, in any body of sacred narrative certain segments of text will be more frequently used to guide and justify behavior. In this case the text justifies differences in the social position of men and women and as such is a "script for power" (Sanday 1981). The idea of key text is especially useful for understanding the complex relationships between different kinds of believers in a community like Ridge County.

Social differentiation of males and females, apparent in most social contexts, is clearest among older people. An especially high degree of role segregation can be found among those engaged in farming rather than industrial employment. While it is absolutely true that women do farm labor, there are few tasks that are clearly interchangeable. The formal political structure of the county has been largely male throughout its history, although there was a female superintendent of schools in the early part of the century. Role segregation is also very strong in the religious life of the county.

Both men and women play important roles in all churches, but there are some interesting patterns of social differentiation. Some churches restrict female participation in ritual to preparing communion, playing the piano or organ, or singing. Women are not invited to offer prayer, serve communion, or preach. Some Holiness churches, however, involve women in all these activities. Even churches that restrict female participation are relaxing the strict segregation of former times. Until recently some churches maintained separate male and female Bible school classes even for elderly people. Some older abandoned church buildings had two front doors, which some report as being for males and females.

Looking back over field notes from the earliest stages of fieldwork, before I was much involved in interviewing or participation, I was struck by how rarely I saw women outside. I hardly ever saw a woman passing the time on a front porch or "loafing" on one of the wooden benches in front of the barber shop or the restaurant in town. At church the men linger outside until time for Bible school or the "preaching service" but women go inside as soon as they arrive. Later, I was aware of the very low participation of males in indoor senior citizens programs and of the special effort that had to be made to have them attend. It is legitimate to suggest that the social world of men is outside and that of women is inside. And of their life after retirement one might say, figuratively, that men retire to the porch and women to the hearth.

Historically the pattern of separation seems to have been even stronger. In interviews that attempted to reconstruct the role of older people in social life at an earlier time it was quite clear that this "inside" and "outside" pattern held true. Men worked in the fields, women in the kitchen. There were conditions under which these boundaries could be crossed, but not many.

While males may have prepared food in the kitchen in emergency circumstances, their food preparation was generally limited to outdoor cooking—fish frying in the old days, charcoal grilling more recently. The fish frying seems to be a carry-over from male-only fish camps, where men prepared their own fish and hush puppies in cast-iron skillets. Even now, when male-dominated voluntary associations sell food to raise money, they tend to have fish fries. Female-dominated organizations sell chili, baked goods, or ham sandwiches. In the few observed cases, surplus food from these events was distributed to old men.

The relationship between women and farm work is much more complex. Women used to perform considerable agricultural labor. Although they virtually never prepared fields with plow and harrow or harvested row crops, they were often intensely involved in dairy herd management and contributed substantially to housing and preparing tobacco for market. I have heard of only one case in which a women actually cut tobacco. Other tasks they may have done are too numerous to list. For the most part women's participation was clearly structured. Most important was the preparation of food for the farm laborers. Women did not usually operate machinery or house tobacco, except to help in "handing off" the wagon or loading the tobacco onto the wagon. Women did frequently "drop plants," which is to say they rode the mechanical setting machine, feeding the plants into it for planting. Women did a great deal of tobacco stripping but would not usually "press" or "bulk" tobacco. Nor would they usually take products to market. Women also worked alongside men in the twice-daily milking of dairy herds if they were not employed in a wage or salary job. They frequently cared for newborn or sick calves in dairy and beef operations.

This apparently strict segregation of male and female roles is maintained partly through training and diffuse ridicule, especially of men who cook. Cooking is considered unmanly. Widowed males are never ridiculed for cooking, but much of the neighborly assistance offered them is in the form of cooked food. In all observed cases such aid was directed at single males of marrying age. Women who do not cook for their husbands are also ridiculed. It would appear that there is a significant cohort effect in role segregation. As more women go to work for wages or salary, men have to shoulder more of the household responsibility, and the segregation is declining in intensity.

As men aged and their capacity for fieldwork declined, their work brought them closer to the house. Withdrawal from work left them literally on the porch. Women's withdrawal from work merely reduced their involvement in fieldwork, which was generally viewed as inappropriate in the first place. While men retired to the porch women remained in the realm that was appropriate to the cultural view of them, the hearth. The implications in a community that places such a high value on work and individual independence are substantial. Men are left with few appropriate alternatives, but women continue to do the work that they have always done.

Some women even do what is generally regarded as men's work. There are older women who derive a significant portion of their income from farming. One in her mid-sixties had been raising "turn-out" cattle for fifteen years, doing a large share of the work herself, although, she said, it was an "uphill battle for a woman alone." Turn-out cattle, a by-product of dairy herds, are bull calves and surplus heifers. They need a lot of attention at first, because they have not been weaned, but they are cheap to buy and hardy once they get on grass. These animals required less work because they were bought as feeders. They were sold once they reached a weight of four or five hundred pounds.

Network size varies with age but in an unanticipated way. The evidence suggests that the postretirement period in Ridge County is a period of social growth. With advancing age, however, the networks shrink once again, declining to preretirement size in the 75-79 age cohort.

Networks can be thought of as having a fundamental core and a supplementary periphery. As they grow, the core tends to remain constant while the periphery expands. To the base of long-duration, high-frequency relationships, individuals tend to add instrumental, shorter-duration, lower-frequency relationships.

The networks of males and females are of equal size, but they differ in the proportions of cross-sex and same-sex relationships. Later in life, males tend to retain a higher percentage of cross-sex relationships, whereas females tend to develop more same-sex relationships.

6. Network Exchange

Porter and Ruby turned into their driveway. Ruby turned out of the seat of the Ford pickup, being careful not to snag her nylons, purposefully strode up the graveled drive, and disappeared into the house. By habit, Porter stopped to see if everything was in order. The newly weaned bull calf stood listlessly in the paddock as if resigned to his pickup truck ride in the morning. Porter knew that Ruby would be doctoring the two new heifers after the dishes. They had invited guests for dinner, Ruby's brother and his new lady friend.

Sunday dinner is the most elaborate meal of the week. Ruby's preparations had started early that morning after she and Porter finished the milking, washed up, and had a second cup of coffee. Most everything was done before they headed toward the Riverton Christian Church. By the time people get home from church they are usually hungry. Sometimes, as was true this day, there are places to go to in the afternoon, and except for the milking they tried to avoid working on the Lord's Day. During the church service someone had "made the good declaration" and was going to be baptized in the early afternoon in a farm pond on the way to town.

They liked to have guests, partly because Ruby set such a nice table, and Porter liked to brag on her. He engaged the guests in conversation while Ruby, at the sideboard, began to cut lard into the flour that she had put without measuring into a white enamel pudding pan. Porter said something about his wife's biscuits. Deftly she turned out the dough, and rolled and cut the biscuits. The already-larded baking pan was pulled from the hot oven, smoking ever so slightly. Ruby looked up and said, "This is the secret," as she first dipped the cut biscuit in the hot fat and then turned it on its bottom. With a you'll-love-'em look in her eye, she explained, "The top browns up real good."

It was a typical Sunday dinner. On the table were home-churned butter and wild plum preserves to accompany the biscuits. The meat was skillet-fried home-raised chicken. It was served with home-canned green beans, cooked with sugar and cured meat for an hour that morning. The home-raised green beans are often varieties like white half-runners that tolerate longer cooking times. Ruby also served boiled potatoes and corn on the cob, which was described as horse corn—that is, it was not "roasting ears," or sweet corn. The meal also included cole slaw with dressing, sliced tomatoes, and some gelatin salad topped with miniature marshmallows.

All but Ruby were seated when Porter asked one of the guests to "return thanks." Perhaps knowing Porter was an elder at the church, the guest declined. So Porter, with eyes closed, began, "Dear precious heavenly Father, we thank you for what we are about to receive. May it nourish us in body and spirit. May you bless the hands that prepared it. And bless those that are here in Christian fellowship. Amen."

The pattern of this meal exhibits some of the basic foodways of the community. All the food is prepared and served by a woman. Meat is deemphasized in favor of a large number of vegetable dishes, and the meat used is fried rather than roasted. The cook uses as much home-produced food as possible. And of course, the meal is more than the food eaten; it is also a kind of sacred ritual. It is the most frequently reported exchange relationship in Ridge County. Participants in the meal are bound together briefly in fellowship and pleasure, and those who receive the gift of food are also bound in time.

Simply put, social networks are exchanges of value between persons. Cognitively, networks are little more than the memory of past exchanges and the anticipation of future exchanges, placed in the context of meaning characteristic of the community. These cognitions seem to be composed of a concatenation of some generalized expectations about how persons in various social categories should act and vague mental accounts that reflect a diffuse history of the reciprocal exchange of value between parties. In the context of kin, friend, and neighbor, diffuseness is characteristic, although not a strict requirement. In his classic

essay, *The Gift*, Marcel Mauss established the importance of exchange to social solidarity (1954). Social action is exchange, the
memory of past transactions form many of the basic meanings.

Our comprehension of these processes is limited because of
the complexity and obscurity of human decision making and
choice in this area of life. How people actually think about exchange in these circumstances is not well documented. Undoubtedly decision making reflects concern with utility, but it
is unclear how salient this dimension is, even in market exchange
(Quinn 1978; Plattner 1974). One can only agree with Vern L.
Bengston and James J. Dowd when they state, "Social behavior
cannot be explained simply by the identification of certain profits
inherent in a course of action" (1980:63). In any case, it is necessary for us to think of relationships in terms of accounts. Participants use the discipline and the quality of the exchange
relationship for evaluation in deciding whether to continue it.

One informant's statement expresses this quality of the process: "A good neighbor is someone you can depend on whenever
you need him. They don't mislead you, let you down. . . . A
new person has to prove hisself. You don't know whether
they're dependable, and they don't know if you are. If you go
and act the part of the neighbor yourself, you can see what the
reaction is, whether it was worth pursuing or whether they were
good, substantial, dependable people. People can let you down
once or twice, but after a while . . . you don't turn the other
cheek." A conversation with a man in his nineties revealed a
specific example of the mechanism in an interaction he reported.
He made an oral agreement with a neighbor to buy some corn
for $1.50 a bushel, including delivery. The neighbor never de-
livered the corn, ostensibly because he was too busy, and the
older farmer was forced to borrow a portion of the corn from
another neighbor pending delivery from the first source. There
was still no delivery and finally the older farmer went to the
second neighbor to pay for the borrowed corn. In the meantime
the price of corn had gone up, and he had to offer $2.25 a bushel,
of which the neighbor only accepted $2.00. The old farmer then
went to see an acquaintance of the man with whom he had made
the original agreement. This man said that the first source would
deliver, but the price would have to be $2.25 a bushel. In the
aftermath the two persons did not exactly stop talking with each

other, but their visits ceased. The old farmer conveyed the idea that he did not like people to go back on their word.

All sorts of things can be exchanged. After a substantial amount of key informant interviewing and participant observation, I identified eight exchange categories for analysis: providing meals, giving gifts of food or drink, giving gifts, providing care when sick, providing labor at no cost, lending tools or other objects, shopping for the person, and providing jobs for pay. In addition, conversation forms an exchange category. Only those with whom ego communicated could be listed in ego's network. Of course, speech contains many things of great value: technical information, humor, affection, reassurance, and relief from boredom. This analysis focuses upon the other categories, however.

The eight exchange categories largely exist outside the market economy and operate in terms of generalized reciprocity (Sahlins 1972). That is, the exchanges do not involve direct and immediate calculations of value more or less equivalent to what anyone would pay for service or goods in the marketplace.[1] In generalized reciprocity exchange the payment in the return is unspecified, unassured, and unscheduled but expected. It is the expectation that binds people—the giver to the future, the receiver to the past.

The interview schedule asked whether a particular exchange behavior was present or absent in the relationship, and information was collected on both giving and receiving behavior. All information was collected from the ego, there was no attempt to cross-check the information from an alter's perspective. No data were collected on the relative amounts exchanged.

The interview experience revealed that the exchange categories selected were culturally appropriate. The behaviors listed in the interview schedule more or less effectively delineated the

1. It is important to note that the boundary between market and nonmarket transactions is not absolutely clear. There are a number of composite transactions, which combine features of both market and nonmarket exchange, including concessionary prices to friends and relatives, especially for land; wage payments to children and other close kin to "help them out," decisions to sell labor to kin or neighbors in preference to others; and many other marketlike transactions that also contain a "different" calculation of value.

Table 6. Frequency and Number of Exchange Relationships

	Given by Ego		Received by Ego			Net
	Number	Percentage	Number	Percentage	Total	Difference
Meals	971	27.98	786	22.65	1,757	+5.33
Gifts	743	21.41	771	22.22	1,514	−0.81
Food	743	21.41	698	20.12	1,441	+1.29
Care	586	16.89	685	19.74	1,271	−2.85
Work	239	6.89	326	9.39	565	−2.50
Shopping	144	4.15	190	5.48	334	−1.33
Lending	152	4.38	129	3.72	281	+0.66
Jobs	84	2.42	65	1.87	149	+0.55

range of behaviors that formed the naturally occurring system of social supports in a reciprocal framework. In effect, what was measured was difference in exchange patterns by age and other dimensions. It was apparent and predictable that there has been considerable secular change in exchange behavior. The network inventory did not measure secular change, but it was apparent in the ethnographic data. In the network interviews, research subjects frequently noted exchanges they "used to" make but not any more. Behavior had altered because of both secular change and aging.

In the most frequent exchange relationship, egos provide meals to alters. Almost 28 percent of ego-alter relationships (971 of them) involved the provision of meals (see Table 6). The second most frequent relationship is the reciprocal, provision of meals by alters. Almost 23 percent of the relationships reported in the interviews (786 of them) were characterized by this kind of exchange. Included were routine family meals as well as special occasions.

Gift giving of various kinds is another frequent exchange relationship, and food and gifts are given with similar frequency. Receiving gifts from alters was the third most frequent exchange relationship, but all forms of gift giving are well represented. Gift giving, of course, focuses on birthdays and Christmas, and gifts can be anything from inexpensive items to family heirlooms. Gifts of food most commonly take the form of garden produce and baked goods. People often contribute prepared dishes during illness, or at funerals, weddings, and other special events. Some cooks specialize in a particular dish, and are expected to bring that dish under many circumstances. Others will refrain from preparing this dish because it is another's prerogative.

Garden produce is often the basis of exchange relationships. Gifts of early produce, such as tomatoes, may be presented to friends and neighbors; late crop surpluses are often shared with those who are active food preservers. Garden produce is almost never sold. Instead, extra produce that cannot be used up or preserved is given away. Even during the Great Depression, when cash was badly needed, Ridge Countians followed this pattern. People may put a bushel or two of vegetables in their pickup truck to give to people as they leave church. Planting decisions may also reflect the practice of network exchange. Some gardeners, for example, plant an extra large crop or grow special commodities. One observed case involved the planting of a very large flower garden, which included peonies, gladiolus, dahlias, chrysanthemums, snapdragons, and petunias. The gardener provides flowers much of the year for his church, and he also gives flowers to friends who want to make "table arrangements." Another gardener grows popcorn for exchange relationships. Sometimes people allow others to use a garden plot, a practice that increases interaction a great deal because of the frequent visits to weed and harvest produce when the garden "comes on." The lender might speak pridefully about the amount of produce grown by others in the garden.

Care giving—preparing meals, doing chores, simple home nursing—is also quite common. Almost 17 percent of the egos provide care to sick neighbors and friends, and they receive such care even more often. A behavior that is also related to health problems is hospital visitation.

Work sharing, help with shopping, lending and borrowing of tools and implements, and hiring people all have a distinctly lower frequency than the other exchanges. Even so, it is important to remember that the total number of alters is about 3,500, yet the number of egos is 139.

Work sharing can develop because one person in the network owns a necessary piece of equipment or because working with others lightens the load. Some tasks are difficult or impossible to perform alone, or an individual may have a disability that makes a job too difficult to accomplish. In one observed case a farmer was not able to spray "sucker dope" on tobacco after topping because wearing a back-pack manual sprayer hurt his back. The farmer himself paid for the "sucker dope," helped mix it, and transported his neighbor to the field. After the spraying was done the farmer with the back problem bought refreshments at the store and left some homegrown apples. Later the farmer with the back problem would reciprocate by helping the other man house his tobacco. During the planning and completion of the task this reciprocation was never discussed. The sprayer was careful to have the other farmer make the decisions about whether the spraying should take place despite the threat of rain, which would diminish the effects of the spraying.

Women also exchange work, most often helping each other at canning time. Canning is hard and hot work and made more pleasant when the work is shared. But work sharing increases the work load of a woman, for she must feed those who are helping. "Feeding the hands" displays a couple's hospitality, and so meals in these settings are often very elaborate, requiring substantial preparation time. The effect is that if men share work, women share it also. One couple in their seventies had worked it out with those who shared that everybody went home for lunch so the women could rest.

Work sharing, lending and borrowing, and hiring people are all subject to the complex patterns of historical change discussed earlier. All three types of exchange are less common than in the past.

Using the X^2 test, analysis shows a higher than expected number of exchange relationships among kin. Meal sharing, food gifts, other gifts, care giving, work sharing and shopping were all more numerous between kin than between non-kin.[2] Egos

2. I used the X^2 test of independence (SAS Institute 1985:948). In the case of meals, gifts, gifts of food, care, work sharing, and shopping the demonstrated difference between kin and nonkin was at the .0001 level of probability. The hiring of kin by egos was more frequent than the hiring of nonkin, at the .0018 level of probability. Egos tended to lend things to kin more than nonkin, at the .005 level of probability. Ego's borrowing from kin was at the .8377 level of probability and hiring of kin was at the .5069 level.

were hired more frequently by kin than by nonkin, and they tended to lend things to kin more frequently than to nonkin. The only two exchange relationships that were not relatively more frequent with kin than nonkin were hiring and borrowing by the egos. In both cases there was no special tendency to hire or borrow things from kin. It is important not to forget that kin often work for cash or some other specified material considera- tion. For example, in one family the younger children who helped with the tobacco housing were paid cash, and the older married children got a butchered hog. Kin may be paid less or they may be paid more than nonkin. The important aspect of the transaction is the labor itself. Labor is scarce, and sometimes it is only the special consideration associated with kinship that enables a farmer to get any help at all. It is not a matter of hiring kin as much as kin consenting to work. In this case we can see how the market structures nonmarket relationships.

The relationship with alters classified as neighbors is different from the relationship with kin. Borrowing and lending are more common with neighbors than with other types of alters. Ex- change of meals is relatively less frequent with neighbors, whereas it is higher with kin. Gifts of food are more likely with neighbors than with other alters, but there are relatively fewer exchanges of other gifts among neighbors. The analysis of care giving suggests that neighbors are both sources and recipients although the relationship is not as strong as with alters that are kin. Egos tend to hire neighbors to a relatively greater extent, but they are hired less frequently by neighbors than by kin. Work sharing among neighbors is more common than would be ex- pected.

Historically, the most significant change in network exchange is in the amount of work sharing between neighbors. The picture of the relationships between neighbors provided by older in- formants is one of consistent, economically significant coopera- tion. Many kinds of activities were carried out together, each calling for a different mix of relationships based on the organi- zational scale appropriate to the task and the nature of the farm- ing operation. Some of the feeling of these relationships is provided in an excerpt from field notes.

We'd, work together in our crops . . . In the fall we'd get up huge piles of wood. We'd have a cut-off saw. We'd use a tractor. Even before the tractor we had a Model-T Ford we'd fix and have a saw pulley on it. We'd go through the neighborhood and each neighbor would help [his] neighbor saw up his winter supply of wood. Maybe we'd take 6 hours, 8 hours, or 10 hours sawing wood. Well, it was just like in the old-fashioned times . . . Before, we'd combine our grain. We'd cut the wheat with the binder . . . that was horses in the binder. Then whenever we'd get ready to thresh, the thresher would come through the community and thresh everybody's wheat. And that's when we'd all get together. . . . We'd maybe have eighteen or twenty different neighbors would come in and help thresh each other's wheat. Same thing when we'd kill hogs. Now this place [here] used to be a main place. Maybe there'd be three or four neighbors here. We'd kill our hogs. They'd bring three hogs and we'd kill, butcher all the hogs in one place.

This level of work sharing and the number of different activities reported have been dramatically reduced. Barn and house raisings, cornhusking, sorghum molasses making, and other collaborative activities were completely abandoned, although some of these activities are being revived. Nowadays those who do such work are usually adults with families, who seem to be motivated by the pleasure of the activity and the nostalgia for earlier days that it evokes. Work sharing does occur, but the size of the groups working is much smaller. Usually not more than two or perhaps three people participate. Only a portion of this work is routine collaboration. Mostly people share work only when someone is in needy circumstances, but the capacity to help in this way is reported to be substantial.

Many people regret the loss of work sharing. Their accounts of this cooperation were expressed in positive, even idealized terms, and they tend to view the decrease in work sharing as a kind of degeneration of human life. Some informants have insisted that in their neighborhoods *no* such cooperation exists. Despite the willingness of some people to believe that the practice has ended because people have weaker character nowadays, it is clear that a number of external factors made work sharing uneconomical while technological change made it less necessary. Rural industrialization played an important role. Farmers with industrial jobs could not allocate time to this kind of activity. Further, an increasing number of neighbors are not farmers at all, and there has been a tendency for the size of farms to increase. With larger operations it is difficult to engage in equitable work exchanges, and consequently the work crew has shifted to "hired hands." Finally, machines and other technological innovations have reduced the need for large work crews. Hay making provides a striking example. Earlier this century the standard technology was the horse-drawn "sickle bar," used in conjunction with the rake and employing a great deal of hand labor. Following World War II, power balers were added to the typical inventory of machines used on Ridge County farms. These machines produced what are locally called square bales and still required a sizable crew of loaders. Recently "hay rollers" have been introduced, which allow one man on a tractor to produce large round bales that can be stored in the field. This shift manifests a common pattern of the substitution of capital for labor, machines for the cooperation of social networks. Similarly, home freezers substitute for cooperative meat butchering and preservation, grain combines for cooperative threshing, chain saws for cooperative wood cutting, and combines for cooperative cornhuskings. Yet, although these innovations have contributed to the decline in work sharing, the important cause is the increased cost of the farmer's labor. It is simply cheaper to hold an industrial job and to hire replacements at the going agricultural labor rate. Industrial jobs discourage the sharing of equipment between neighbors. Moreover, ownership gives independence and control over work by obviating the need to coordinate work with neighbors. Those involved in wage labor lose their capacity to critically time their farm work. Crops are planted when there is time, not when growing conditions are optimal.

Improved access to retail outlets has decreased petty borrowing among neighbors. One person noted, "Anymore, people don't borrow like they used to. You never hear of it no more, or least I don't never hear of it. I reckon it's because we're all so close to town and can run and get it."

And historical transformations in health care are substantial, as well. While primary health care was available from a physician from the earliest days of the county's existence, informants report that much care was provided at home. Few births, for example, took place in the hospital. Kin were expected to care for the sick. One informant said flatly, "It was the child's obligation to take care of the parents during their old age, as the parents had taken care of them when they were helpless."

The exchange relationships manifest asymmetry, which I will consider at the aggregate level and at the level of the individual. Asymmetry is predictable on methodological grounds, and one might expect that egos would report more giving than receiving relationships, overreporting their own generosity. Alternatively, on theoretical grounds one might expect that the alters, supporting an aging, "dependent" population would be involved in more giving relationships than taking.

The examination of frequency of exchange relationships presented in Table 6.1 demonstrates the basic asymmetry of exchange at the community level. These figures are based on examination of all the aggregated alters. The percentages reported represent the number of all alters with whom the egos reported a specific exchange relationship. The exchange categories are ranked in terms of total number of exchange relationships of the type, adding both giving and receiving relationships. The percentage of receiving relationships was subtracted from the percentage of giving relationships to produce the net difference. It is important to remember that the figures represent exchange relationships, not individual people. An ego could have up to eight exchange relationships with a single alter and as few as zero.

The pattern of asymmetry appears in comparing the total number of giving relationships with the total number of receiving relationships in each exchange category. The asymmetry can be either negative or positive, depending on the exchange category. Egos are more likely to give their alters meals, food gifts, and jobs and lend them tools than to receive these benefits from their alters. They are less likely than their alters to give

gifts, care, free labor, and shopping services. A more fundamental pattern is shown when we compare relationships associated with goods and those associated with services. Egos, it is
clear, are "net givers" in terms of goods or money and "net
receivers" of services. The egos enter into more goods-giving
relationships, with the exception of gifts. If we add the net differences between numbers of giving and receiving relationships
among the goods and services subsets of exchange relationships
(meals, gifts, food gifts, lending, and jobs) and calculate the
mean, we find that on the average the persons in the network
sample enter into 48.8 more goods giving relationships than
goods-receiving relationships with their alters. In contrast the
mean difference between giving and receiving service relationships (care, work sharing, and shopping) that they enter is negative number, -77.3.

An exchange symmetry score was calculated for individual
egos.[3] The score was derived from a formula that subtracted
receiving relationships from giving relationships, summed these
and divided by the total possible relationships. A symmetrical
relationship would result in the score of zero. The scores could
theoretically range from plus one (all giving) to minus one (all
receiving). The actual range was $+.2202$ to $-.3333$ and the mean
was $-.0011$. The mode was 0.000.

There are some significant differences in exchange symmetry
between the various age groups.[4] The mean exchange symmetry

---

3. Exchange symmetry was calculated by the following formula: $(Mg - Mr) + (Fg - Fr) + (Gg - Gr) + (Cg - Cr) + (Hg - Hr) + (Wg - Wr) + (Sg - Sr) + (Lg - Lr)/8$ where: Mg = a meal giving relationship; Mr = a meal receiving relationship; Fg = a food giving relationship; Fr = a food receiving relationship; Gg = a gift giving relationship; Gr = a gift receiving relationship; Cg = a care giving relationship; Cr = a care giving relationship; Hg = a job giving relationship; Hr = a job receiving relationship; Wg = a work giving relationship; Wr = a work receiving relationship; Lg = a lending relationship; Lr = a borrowing relationship. A complete receiver would have a score of -1.00 and a complete giver would have a score of $+1.00$. Even giving and receiving would be 0.00.

4. Examinations of the relationships between various categories (i.e., age, sex) were accomplished using the Student-Newman-Keuls test of the General Linear Models Procedure in SAS.

Table 7. The Relationship Between Age Grouping and Exchange Symmetry Score

	Score	Number
60-64	+ .007	665
65-69	+ .019	966
70-74	− .012	655
75-79	− .023	666
80	− .034	513

Note: F value 21.46, Prob. = 0.0001

scores for individuals 70 years old and older strata were negative. The most negative mean symmetry score of all five strata was the 80 and older category. The age strata 60-64 and 65-69 were characterized by positive symmetry scores. The most positive symmetry score was for the individuals in the 65-69 age stratum. The age stratum with the largest network had the most positive symmetry score (i.e. more giving relationships).

While the relationship between age and exchange symmetry is significant it is not as linear as I had expected. I had posited a simple negative relationship between age and exchange symmetry. The appearance of the 65-69 stratum as the most positive is inconsistent with the expected linear pattern but follows the general pattern associated with this age stratum in this study. This group has larger networks than any other age stratum. Apparently those who fall within its bounds are capable of engaging in more giving relationships than others studied. It seems that these people, more apt to be free of work responsibilities than those 60-64 and less likely to be disabled or uninterested than their seniors, have the capacity and desire to enter into network relationships. The predicted linear pattern was not found in the middle age strata. The position of the oldest age stratum is strongly consistent with the predicted linear pattern (see Table 7).

The mean exchange symmetry score of females is positive, and the score for males is negative. The difference is not significant, but it is inconsistent with the prediction that males would have significantly more positive scores than females. As

Table 8. The Relationship Between Age Grouping and Exchange
Complexity

60-64	.144
65-69	.131
70-74	.110
75-79	.131
80>	.143

Note: $F = 16.61$, Prob $= 0.0001$

I anticipated, neither kinship status or sex of alters was related
to significant differences in this score.

I also analyzed exchange relationships without regard to exchange symmetry, using a similar strategy. In this case, however, I simply added the categories (rather than subtracting the
receiving relationships from the giving relationships) and divided by the total possible number of relationships. A network
that consisted of all receiving relationships would be as complex
as a network that consisted of all giving relationships. Of course
the same networks would have symmetry scores at the opposite
ends of the possible range. What is called complexity is similar
to the classic network content variable expressed as uniplexity
and multiplexity. Both complexity and multiplexity are based on
numbers of relationships but complexity represents interval
rather than nominal data.

The relationship between age and network complexity is curvilinear, best described as a U-shaped distribution (see Table 8).
The most complex relationships are to be found in the youngest
and oldest age strata, whereas the lowest mean complexity score,
significantly lower than the others, is in the 70 to 75 age strata.
The other strata are intermediate.

In this analysis women's networks were characterized by significantly more complex exchange relationships than men's.
That is, female egos activated more different kinds of relationships, whether positive or negative (male ego, .114; female ego,
.147). Relationships with alters who are kin are very much more
complex (relatives, .225; nonrelatives, .068), but the sex of the
alter was not significant (male alters, .126; female alters 0.135).
Relationships with people classified as friends were not more

complex than those with people not classified in this way (friend, .132; nonfriend, .114). Relationships with best friends were more complex (best friend, .257; not best friend, .124). Exchange relationships of the persons who reported themselves as not retired were more complex. Significance of these scores was determined by the t test.

Field observation and interviews identified a number of different exchange relationships, which proved to be representative of a major segment of the nonmarket exchange relationships of the study population. The behavior represented by these categories was subject to both life-course change and secular change.

Analysis of aggregate exchange relationship data demonstrates that those interviewed enter into more relationships within which they give than relationships in which they receive. While one might assume that this finding is a product of a tendency for persons to overreport their generosity, further analysis reveals a basic pattern of asymmetry in types of exchange. That is, among these people there is an apparent flow of goods from them and services to them.

Analysis of the data at an individual level reveals some age-related differences in exchange symmetry and complexity. The expected linear negative relationship was found only in a general sense. Persons in age strata below seventy years of age were "net givers," and those above were "net receivers." While the oldest age stratum had the most negative exchange score, the youngest age stratum was not the most positive. The persons in the 65-69 age strata entered into the largest surplus of giving relationships. The analysis of complexity revealed a curvilinear relationship between age and complexity, in which the oldest and the youngest persons had the most complex relationships.

7. Old Friends and Perfect Strangers

Social organization is the outcome of choice expressed through social structures, conditioned by history and environment. This research addresses the social network aspect of the social organization of older people living in Ridge County. The foundation is a body of analyzed social network data coupled with selected ethnographic and culture history data from the community studied and a comparison with conceptually similar studies carried out in other American communities. These data support research conclusions in three areas. The first is the nature of social networks of older people in a single community with commentary on life-course changes as approximated through cross-sectional data. The second area is the social effects of historical processes of change that structure social life in the community. Third, the research, in conjunction with comparison of other studies, supports conclusions about how macrolevel structural economic factors affect the social life of older people. The three analyses produced a set of highly congruent conclusions associated with the political economy.

The older people of Ridge County of different ages experience differences in their social relationships. There is a general trend toward reduction in the size of social networks, but those in the youngest stratum have much smaller networks than those in the next stratum, whose networks are by far the largest. In later years a linear decline is apparent. This curvilinear pattern suggests, among other things, that researchers concerned with the late-life decline in social involvement of older people need to consider it in a wider age range. In Ridge County people are most involved socially in their late sixties and early seventies. While the oldest people in the study have the smallest social networks, they are comparable in size to those of the youngest stratum. We must, therefore, ask ourselves if the late-life decrease in social involvement, around which much social gerontological theory has centered, merely represents readjustment to a previous pattern after a late life florescence of social relationships.

It is analytically inappropriate to think of these older people as dependent, for they are important sources of "social support," important providers in their relationships. The ethnographic data show that much aid for the old is given by the old themselves, people in their fifties, sixties, and seventies. This segment of the population bears substantial responsibility for familial and church-based supportive behavior directed at the needs of older people. The same conclusion is borne out by the network data itself. Younger constituents of the sample entered into more giving relationships, whereas those above seventy tended to enter into more receiving relationships, and those in the oldest strata were the most strongly defined receivers of all. Clearly, it would be misleading to speak of "social support" in the context of older people without accounting for this self-supportive behavior.

Aggregating the exchange data reveals underlying community exchange structures. Evidence derived from analysis of the numbers and types of relationships into which people enter shows that there is a flow of goods from the sample in return for services from network alters. If analysis of relationships is an indicator, social aging involves the exchange of goods for services. This result is consistent with the analysis of landownership and use in rural Illinois done by Sonya Salamon and Vicki Lockhart (1980). Historically, it appears, the rural elderly, particularly farm owners, have traded land or access to land for support in old age (Homans 1941, Arensberg and Kimball 1968). Social aging is marked by divestment of property.

The term *social aging* deserves some explanation. Vern L. Bengtson (1973) used the term to focus on the developmental events in a person's lifetime as a conceptual substitute for chronological age. As Bengston explains, "It is crucial to recognize that we are not talking about chronological age but about events which are linked to the passage of time" (1973:8). Social aging is based on the accumulation of social events, defined by Bengston as the "entrance and the exit from the major areas of social interaction in life—marriage, work, parenting, social organization" (1973:9). Social organization in this context must bear a narrower meaning than it does in this book. Bengston's concept of social aging stresses the various arenas of social interaction. His idea, which seems to be largely ignored, could be used as a foundation for developing an understanding of the social lives of older people. Speaking schematically, it may be useful to develop a concept of social aging that focuses on the manifested aspects of social behavior, such as life-course changes in network size. It is necessary to compile extensive data on social interaction from various segments of the population at various ages, perhaps in coordination with the "events" to which Bengston refers. This would allow development of a comparative data base on the relationship between age and social behavior. Because of the high transferability of the network concept it would be useful to use this concept as a point for collecting data. The focus should be a developmental consideration of the entire life course.

In contrast to Bengston's conception I would prefer to conceive of the process of social aging as less staged. I think that the establishment of the goal of describing life-course changes in social organization would significantly benefit the development of social gerontology theory. It might serve to allow some growth through synthesis by giving researchers the opportunity to look beyond the contentious, theories-in-conflict perspective so often assumed by social gerontologists. Much of the conflict can be avoided by recognizing that the many theories are addressing different aspects of the same phenomenon, that many theories can be true. A descriptive social aging perspective may serve as a ground for building a comprehensive empirical base for a social theory of aging applicable in a variety of cultural or ecological settings.

The data on exchanges support a number of concurrent explanations. First, they are consistent with aspects of an exchange theory of social aging (Dowd 1975, Bengston and Dowd 1980). Those in the oldest age stratum (80 and above) manifest the most negative exchange symmetry scores and the smallest social network. The age stratum with the largest networks (65-69) also has the most positive symmetry scores of any stratum. These results are consistent with the basic proposition of social gerontological exchange theory, that social isolation is associated with diminution of resources (Bengston and Dowd 1980:66). Doris Francis cogently describes the effect of prestige differences on the social relationships of older people in her comparative study of Cleveland, Ohio and Leeds, England (1984:109-11). It is apparent from her account that people will curtail relationships with others if they feel unequal. Jennie Keith shows the mechanisms of status in her study of French retirement residence (1977:66-84) where people conventionally act to limit recognition of wealth and educational differences so as to not inhibit social activities. Exchange theory posits a direct relationship between power, thought of as the capacity to allocate goods and services, and participation in social relationships (Bengston and Dowd 1980:66). Although my results encourage an exchange theory interpretation of social aging, the research did not allow examination of the mechanisms of choice. Vern L. Bengston and James J. Dowd argue that the loss of self-esteem associated with participating in unequal power relationships is the factor that structures the choice to disengage (1980:69). The actual content of decision making was not examined in Ridge County, nor do data relevant to this problem appear in observed natural discourse very often there. Social inequality is simply not emphasized in discourse. For example, the clear socioeconomic status differences between Holiness and mainline church congregations was rarely alluded to and in some contexts denied. In my documentation of community norms, it became apparent that power is a component of the relationships but that these relationships are quite heavily conditioned by community propensity to limit or mask power differences. The evidence for inequality is nevertheless substantial in Ridge County. There were, for example, a few black families living in the county until sometime in the 1950s, apparently a remnant of the small nineteenth-century slave population. In addition, there have always been tenant farmers, although the percentage of farms operated by tenants has declined to about one-third of historical levels. It is important to note that tenancy rates reported in census materials include not only sharecroppers but also people who are using tenancy to expand production or to start the process of becoming landowners. Community leaders resisted the use of eligibility requirements in some federal programs. There are farmers with substantial net worth, perhaps a million dollars, yet this wealth is not obvious from their consumption and display of goods, and even though these people can be thought of as wealthy, their assets are not especially liquid and their cash flow may be quite limited.

The general deemphasis of inequality resonates with the normative Arminianist theology of county churches, all of which stress the importance of individual faith rather than good works for salvation. Thus, the ultimate existential problem is dealt with in an egalitarian mode, more or less continually restated from the pulpit. To be sure the person who attends a Holiness church is typically much less well off than his or her brothers and sisters in the old-line churches. Nevertheless all churchgoers hear the message of equality preached by respected, authoritative persons. The egalitarian ideology of faith-based salvation can be interpreted as an important structural element in the social organization of Ridge County. Of course, there is no question that social inequality structures social relationships. It is just that the ideology does not support it. It is likely that this component of community ideology serves to limit the social isolation of old people.

Understanding the material basis of Ridge County life and its changing nature is necessary for understanding the social organization of older people in the county. The general process of change can be thought of as composed of subprocesses, which are apparent in the history of Ridge County (Bennett 1976). These subprocesses—agricultural intensification, population decrease, commoditization of production, market penetration, delocalization, and increased regulation—relate to many aspects of social life in general and social networks in particular. They should be regarded as a component of the structural conditions under which the choices of social life are made, but not as a constant, influencing everyone equally. Some of the people in the county left, others have just arrived. All are subject to different histories within the same general system. A woman who went to live with her grown son's family in Cincinnati is really part of the total story, as is an older couple who just bought a farm in Ridge County to raise a few fine horses in their early retirement years. Some are insulated from the processes, largely because of the nature of their employment in stable, nonfarm occupations. Others, such as sharecroppers, are more exposed to the effects of the changes. Yet, however differential the effects on the population, these processes clearly affect community life.

During the childhoods of the persons interviewed for the network analysis most Ridge Countians were engaged in a complex form of shifting agriculture. These agriculturalists were supported by such specialists as blacksmiths, saddlers, harness makers, physicians, and schoolteachers, and by others who held various governmental positions. Other local specialists constructed houses and barns. Most households produced most of their own food. Tobacco and, later, dairy products were sold for cash to pay taxes and buy supplies and equipment. Animal traction was used exclusively until the 1920s and extensively into the early 1950s. According to the United States Census only thirteen Ridge County farms (1.6 percent) had tractors in 1930; by 1949, 86 farms (15 percent) had at least one tractor; and by 1959, 230 farms (45.7 percent) had at least one tractor (U.S. Bureau of the Census 1932, 1952, 1961; Arcury, 1983). Mechanization of farming developed slowly because hilly terrain made it unsuitable for some farms. Some older farmers still speak of "tractor farms." The most important energy sources were animal feed raised by the farmer and firewood collected from woodlots. Fossil fuel was used from the beginning of the study period in the form of coal oil for illumination and coal for heat, but it was not until the 1940s that truck and tractor fuel became an important farm input.

In the earlier periods of the study period, farming was not subject to much regulation and control. There were attempts within the region to withhold tobacco production in order to raise the prices received for this important source of cash. The most important such effort, called the Cut-out, was enforced by what are referred to as night riders. The region went through a kind of peasant war, which helped to generate the present tobacco program, involving both government regulation and farmer cooperation (Axton 1975). Later government regulations limited farmer sales of milk and processed foods, such as cured hams and sausage, and mandated sanitary milk storage. In most

cases, when consumer-protection legislation developed in relation to farm products, more older producers chose to stop
producing than younger producers. While ethnographic data
were being collected, people were confronted with the new regulation permitting farmers to bale tobacco rather than tie it into
hands. This provoked discussions of the cost of baling equipment and whether older farmers could get the "good out of the
equipment" before retirement. Acceptance of this innovation
was widespread among older farmers, because it produced a
tremendous reduction in labor for the relatively modest cost of
putting together a baler. Generally, regulation of farm production stimulates a shake-out of smaller and older producers. Older
farmers are more exposed to buffeting by regulatory change because they have less time to amortize new investment and are
forced to discount valuable equipment and facilities.

The dominant goal of the farm households of the earliest period was direct provisioning. Gradually, however, subsistence
farming has given way to a more intense market orientation in
which farmers sell commodities and perform industrial labor to
obtain cash, which was used to provision the households. Although the transition to indirect provisioning is substantial these
people still produce and preserve much of their own food. Gardens are ubiquitous. Beef cattle are often either raised or purchased for household consumption. Livestock auctions see the
sales of small lots of what auctioneers call "meat hogs" for fall
and winter butchering. The movement from subsistence to intense agriculture is probably less rapid and complete than in
agricultural communities dominated by corporate farming, because of the nature of the important cash crop, tobacco. Regulation and agronomic requirements have limited the scale of
production. Tobacco harvesting technology, for instance, has not
changed in any important way since the earliest production in
Virginia in the sixteenth century. The farmer still walks the fields
cutting stalks with a bladed tool. Attempts to mechanize the
harvest have failed because the advantages do not justify the
capital investment. The necessity for hand harvesting limits
economies of scale; small operators experience no competitive
disadvantage, except perhaps from the standpoint of buying
inputs. Moreover, regulations limit the amount of tobacco a single farmer can produce. Most farmland in the burley belt is as-

signed an authorization for the owner to market a certain number of pounds of tobacco within a system of guaranteed minimum prices. Producers can expand production by leasing these authorizations but only within a single county. Because of the history of this program, these allotments tend to be leased by the young from the old. Because of unfavorable market conditions for tobacco relating to chronic oversupply, increased levels of imports and changing views of the governmental role in maintaining price levels for agricultural commodities, the system that includes the marketing quota provisions is being brought into question. If the system is abandoned, great harm will be done to older people in many states in the American Southeast. Their incomes from leasing quotas and their participation in farm management will be reduced, and the value of land tied to tobacco quotas will decline.

Although tobacco production possesses some distinctive features, however, the general pattern described here is largely applicable to all American rural communities over the last century. It is more strongly expressed in Kentucky in the context of farming systems based on specialized grain production. The process is especially evident in the highly industrialized farming of central California so ably described by Walter R. Goldschmidt in *As You Sow* (1947).

Many of the indicators of the transition that appear in the general and agricultural census indicate a gradual transformation over the eighty years of the reference period. The most important census evidence is reduction of the variety of commodities raised on each farm and increase in farm size and use of machinery (Arcury 1983:60-84). Oral testimony and the analysis of the chronology of important changes indicate that many changes grew out of the Depression-era programs and World War II.

A primary effect of this complex shift is loss of rural population, which has decreased the fertility of the remaining population and increased the average age. The population age/sex pyramid has become columnar (Arcury 1983:47-48), as the independent young have moved away, leaving older segments of the population and increasing age segregation, which reduces the level of intergenerational economic cooperation. An important social consequence of the out-migration is the institution of family and church reunions. Church reunions are often called

homecomings. These activities were made possible by the availability of automobiles.

Another primary effect is economic diversification at the community level and a more complex occupational structure. At least
some of the complexity relates to the changes in agriculture and
the way the community is organized. The county becomes a
place of residence for people working in other places, and the
occupational structure of the community as reflected in the census is, thus, a good deal more complex than the community
division of labor (Arcury 1983:51-60). Economic diversification
of agricultural components of the household economies declines
a great deal. Increasingly, people are employed in industry or
as farmers producing commodities for the market or both.

An important effect of these processes is network density
reduction and its consequences. The tendency of people to
"know everybody else" declines as new and unfamiliar people
move into the community and familiar people leave. One
seventy-year-old woman described her perception of the cause
and effects:

> I can tell you how it was when I was living in the prime
> of my life. I knew everyone in Ridge County. I knew who
> their parents were and their grandparents, marriages be-
> tween families. It was just like a large community. But now
> then outsiders are buying up little parcels of land. Lot of
> people moving into the county. . . . Lot of land owned by
> strangers. . . . That has really had not a good effect on the
> county. . . . Ridge County was almost without crime be-
> cause everybody knew everybody else. . . . I know how I
> felt when I was growing up; I had relatives all around me.
> I didn't dare step out of approved conduct because some
> of my relatives were always watching me. You couldn't
> escape from them. But now the people don't have the close-
> ness, and of course that's universal. They don't have the
> sense of integrity and responsibility that they used to feel.
> Your moral codes, your ethics were controlled by the com-
> munity within which you lived and you conform-
> ed. . . . Having lived my seventy-odd years I have seen
> both conditions. I never felt any fear in my early days,
> because I knew nobody was going to harm me. And I

walked the fields in the dark and went out and took care
of the stock in the barn at night. [I went to] see about the
little lambs. I lived entirely without fear. . . . Families grew
up on farms and someone in the family kept the farm. You
never thought you were alone. You were always surrounded by things you had been familiar with all your life.
Even though some people married and gone on some place
else, the majority married other persons from the county.
It has tended to be a very close-knit community. It has
changed quite a bit now.

The social conditions of the past are difficult to reconstruct,
but they certainly included somewhat more labeling and evaluation of members of the community. Speaking of circumstances
in a rural village, one informant noted that her contact with other
children was restricted if their families were negatively evaluated—i.e. if they used alcohol or were dishonest, wasteful, un-
reliable or did not care for children and elderly people within
their membership. The response to such people was social os-
tracism. Neighborly economic cooperation would be limited, as
would other kinds of economic transactions. As people in the
community know each other less, this kind of evaluation becomes less feasible. It becomes especially difficult to monitor
interaction among children to the extent that it was done in the
past. In this respect, the population changes in Ridge County
have worked to open society.

Population changes also contribute to changes in land use.
The outsiders who buy land use it differently from the native
Ridge Countians. Said one informant: "They strip off all that is
valuable. If there is valuable lumber they get rid of that as soon
as possible. They want to make all they can off the acreage rather
than to preserve the fertility of the soil." Other outsiders buy
land for weekend residences and they may not farm at all. Farmland that is left fallow quickly becomes overgrown, with negative
effects on the value of the land and the general economic situation in the county. A bank official expressed concern about,
"land going back to the Abe Lincoln days."

Another major cause of density reduction is industrial employment, which, though it might be viewed as essential in the
cash-flow situation of typical farm households, changes the or-

der of social networks in an important way. By reducing the amount of economic collaboration between neighbors, it inhibits the development of long-term exchange accounts and so reduces social solidarity. These relationships, or accounts, are very durable and to some extent, once established last beyond a person's capacity to keep up his or her end. The supportive nature of the social networks relates to their roots in earlier economic cooperation between friends and neighbors. Relationships formed decades ago are important for preventing social isolation. These relationships formed interpersonally are generalized between families and friends.

The involvement of women in industrial work also leads to the abandonment of traditional craft pursuits, some of which—the quilting bee, for example—were practiced in "network" settings. As one woman who had quilted extensively in the past noted, "That was one of the nice things about community living. The women were not out working a day's work in a factory. In their spare time in the afternoon they would visit and make quilting." Dairying had always been characterized by extensive female participation. It was apparent to one informant who was involved in the dairy industry that female industrial employment led to a reduction in the number of diary operations.

A corollary to density reduction is an increase in age segregation, which has been most apparent from the time of the Depression onward. It is manifested in many social contexts. Perhaps most significant is the decreased participation of older family members in the activities of the farm economy. In former times, people worked as long "as they were able," and there were always plenty of tasks that could be done by older people. As one person mentioned, "A lot of things didn't require a great deal of action or energy. It helped out in small ways." In addition to changing labor patterns, there are now many organizations specifically directed at the young or the old that enhance age segregation. There have also been parallel changes in the school system that have reduced the amount of direct education by grandparents and parents. During the reference period of the study the formal education system developed from one-room schools with a short school year to a single consolidated school for the county. Children are now away from the home for much more time during the year, and they are less subject to parental control.

Industrial employment relates to the creation of "age-graded" voluntary associations. The best example is the newly formed homemakers clubs adapted to the needs of women who are industrially employed. Clubs of this sort organized for farm women customarily met during the day. Women would assemble once a month at the home of one of the members. This schedule was feasible because these farm housewives controlled their time, however hard they had to work. For industrially employed women to participate, however, meetings had to be held in the evening. Now, the industrially employed women, who have a lower average age, meet in the evening, and the older farm wives continue to meet during the day. In one community the night-meeting group is called the "youngtimers."

Age segregation extends to the level of the household, as Thomas A. Arcury demonstrated in his analysis of Ridge County household composition. He found that in 1900 elderly persons, particularly females but also significant numbers of males lived in households not headed by them or their spouses (1986). By 1980 most elderly males and females were household heads, because many of them lived alone.

On the effects of age segregation, one informant commented: "I think children are deprived today. . . . While the parents were too busy to give attention to the children, the grandparents could be that person and listen to the children. . . . I think it is not treating them fairly, I think even as animals. . . . they are exposed to all the different ages. And they learn from each other. I think that children are deprived of a lot of knowledge that they should have because they do not have contact with older people." The interaction between old and young was "natural; it wasn't planned," but age segregation was

doing away with the basics, which help us to be what a human ought to be: the love and the tenderness that is part of this interrelationship between the ages, where you had the grandparents and the great-grandparents and the parents that were with their children. Even parents and children are separated now until children don't learn very much from their parents. And that does away with the feelings of interresponsibility and how I must help make things easier and direct those that are younger than I, and then on the other hand, for young people to be taught respect, concern, and interest in older people to do things that they can, to make life a little easier.

Prior to the late 1930s there seem to have been few social programs specifically geared to the young or to the old. Nowadays, however, there are age-structured voluntary associations, visitation programs at church, and special social service programs. The earliest manifestation is special Sunday school classes for the young. Now all churches have special programs for both old and young.

The labor economy atomizes society. As economic collaboration at the household level declines so does economic collaboration at the neighborhood level. Charles E. Martin discusses such changes in an Appalachian Kentucky neighborhood context, which finally ended in the abandonment of the neighborhood, in his *Hollybush: Folk Building and Social Change in an Appalachian Community* (1984). Similar patterns of historical change have been documented in studies of an Illinois community (Faragher 1985) and a region in Georgia (Hahn 1985). Farming has become more capital intensive as machinery is substituted for labor, and capital for cooperation. Aside from the virtual abandonment of traditional cooperative work and reduced work sharing among neighbors, which are lamented in a generalized way, changes in the labor economy have a vital effect on the position of older people in this community. Mutual aid between kin and neighbors creates obligations that people can draw on throughout the course of their lives. Those who properly engage in the generalized exchange relationships are often able to maintain the relationships even after they lose the ability to reciprocate. Such exchange accounts can be very durable, for exchange has a memory. Moreover, a good history of participation in exchange relationships helps persuade others to enter into giving relationships. Figurative accounts are transferred between generations, shared within families, and subject to a fuzzy awareness in much of the community. The history of exchange relationships between two older people is reflected in the relationships between younger members of the families. The idea of obligation generalizes to other like persons.

The pattern of atomization of labor was thought to extend to the husband and wife relationship. An informant reflecting on her experiences as a farm housewife suggested that the pattern of the farm division of labor prior to the availability of industrial employment made for more stable marital relationships. She asserted that,

> If young couples now have a disagreement, they don't try to overcome it. They just say, "I am not going to put up with that. I'll just cut loose." But when you were partners on the farm, you just didn't do that. Each one needed the other; there was a lot more stability in family life when you were on the farm. When you are holding jobs, you can separate and you can still hold the job. I couldn't have run the farm. And my husband told me if I had died before he did that he would have to get out and look for someone to keep the house because he could not keep the house. So we were very necessary to each other.

Associated with these transformations is increasing delocalization. As noted, the first use of fossil fuel was for illumination and heat. Early newspapers include advertisements for both coal oil and coal, which was apparently shipped downriver from West Virginia mines and landed at an Ohio River port north of Ridge County and at a railhead to the southwest. One informant recollected that the coal was brought to their farmstead on a wagon with a four-horse hitch. One impetus for using coal was increasing scarcity of firewood. The shift from local energy sources to external energy sources is another aspect of shift from social cooperation to mechanization. Mechanization requires external sources of energy. At the beginning of the research reference period, most farm equipment was brought into the county from outside manufacturers. Wagons, plows, and other implements were not made in the county. There was, however, a well-developed equipment-repair industry. Blacksmiths could be found in town and in the rural hamlets. The cooperative relationships farmers once had with neighbors and kin have been usurped by machines, but machines do not return favors.

In this way the formation of enduring exchange relationships is curtailed. The implications of the new economics increase as a person ages, and it becomes more difficult to establish relationships.

Broadening the concept of delocalization somewhat, it is possible to see a shift from local to external sources of services especially relevant to old people. From 1900 until the 1950s primary health care was more or less totally provided within the county. Since the early 1960s, however, almost all primary care was has been provided outside the county, along with secondary and tertiary care, which were always provided outside the community to the extent that they were available. Because there are no nursing homes or other chronic care facilities in the county, many older people are removed from the community and their networks are disrupted.

The market has also penetrated the realm of death and funerals. During earlier periods, the dead were buried by the family in family graveyards. Burials occurred soon after death in those days before embalming and refrigerated storage. The contemporary pattern of delay in the service and burial is in part an accommodation to out-migration and the relatively high mobility of the population that has moved away. The cost of these early funerals was very low, and consequently older people did not have to make special plans. Morticians' services were available in the town from the very beginning of this period.

The transition from a subsistence-dominated to a market-dominated economy also brings changes in values. An informant described the shift in general terms:

> Well, in times past, going back to my early days, people's thoughts weren't centered on getting farther along. People were more contented. And there was not the envy among people. I never heard my parents say that they wished they had what so and so had. . . . We had the essentials and people were contented with the essentials. They didn't have to put someone else down in order to climb a little higher. If your next door neighbor wanted to live a little differently from you, that was all right. . . . When people were self-sufficient there was less tendency to covet things.

In such remarks one can sense a lag between the dominant values of the community and the material conditions of life that individuals face. During their lives, people are both dependent and independent. The crucial questions are when they are dependent and on whom. At the beginning of the reference period dependence on the household was defined as independence. This view expresses a value that appears with great consistency within the community and lends shape to many institutions. People believe that the worth of an individual is based on self-sufficiency, and this value extends as well to groups. Families, neighbors, and church members are expected to provide for their own, to establish the independence of the group. Beyond these relationships, when aid is given or received, it is thought of in different terms and is regarded as a kind of dependency. There is a special relationship between kin, which can be seen in the exchange complexity of this type of ego-alter relationship, but the pattern of aid and cooperation extends beyond kin, forming a kind of "moral familism" in contrast to Edward Banfield's concept of amoral familism (1958). People believe they have a special responsibility toward kin, but they also operate with a well-developed conception of their own universal responsibility. The outer limit of the arena of responsibility seems to be the extent of relationships that operate under a regime of generalized reciprocity. The formation and continuation of these relationships, however, has been curtailed by the processes of transformation. Increasingly, individual needs can be met only by institutions other than kinship, and government and church organizations have come to play a more important role. Relationships with government programs are inconsistent with the values adapted to the earlier agrarian period, but activities of the church are interpreted differently. Of course the resources of the churches are extremely limited in a material sense. They are rarely sources of cash. Nevertheless, their ability to mobilize supportive social interaction is very high. Inevitably, people perceive these aspects of the lag between needs and values as evidence of the evolution of moral defect in society. It is a way to cope with rapid change in the material basis of social life, which has produced so many discrepancies between values developed during the formative period of life and present needs. It is also probably inevitable that in confronting these discrepancies humans see the necessary adaptations as evidence of moral degeneration.

As mentioned earlier, Walter R. Goldschmidt studied a set of communities in the Central Valley of California in the early 1940s to document the social effects of industrialized farming. He characterizes industrialized farming as "intensive cultivation, high per-acre and per-farm capital investment, high specialization in single crops on individual farms, highly mechanized operations, large requirements of wage labor hired on an impersonal basis, and large-scale operations" (1947:187). Although this characterization does not apply to Ridge County in a strict sense, it indicates the direction in which the economy is developing. An examination of some of his conclusions is useful because his study reflects an evolution which is parallel and further along than that found in Ridge County.

While all of the communities Goldschmidt compared had industrialized farming systems, they also varied. One of the communities, Dinuba, included a substantial number of smaller farms along with its large-scale specialized farms. Demographically, about one-third of the households were headed by farmer-owners, a higher number than in other communities more dominated by the industrial farms. These farm-owning households tempered the social effects of agricultural industrialization. Although the community was socially stratified in much the same way as the other communities, Goldschmidt reported that "the lines of cleavage are less sharp and the social distance not so great in Dinuba" as in the other communities. "There is a greater wealth of institutions, a larger and more diversified stable population, and particulary more persons whose social affiliations are determined not by the dominant pecuniary values of urban society but rather by the specific attitudes and ethos of one or another cultural subgroup" (1947:193). Further, within each of the existing subdivisions, everybody knew everybody else. It is also interesting to note that Dinuba had more older people than the other communities, although Goldschmidt considered the higher incidence primarily as a function of the relatively higher age of Dinuba itself. While Dinuba is quite different from Ridge County, it tells us a great deal about the basic issue we are considering here.

The comparison panel of the other social network and aging

studies introduced in Chapter 1 allows us to examine the social life of older people in terms of differences in the structure of the political economy. There are similarities between the communities in these studies and Ridge County. A number of comparable data points are considered here before the differences in network size are considered. The mean age of the Ridge County sample is 72.6 years, with a range of 60 to 97 years. The mean sample age and range of the comparison panel is similar. For the Midtown SRO study, Sokolovsky and Cohen report a mean age of 71.9 years and a range of 60 to 93 years (1978). Eckert reports a mean age of 65.4 years for the West Coast SRO population and a range of 50 to 93 years (1983). In their population of Bowery men, Cohen and Sokolovsky found a mean age of 67.1 years and a range of 60 to 89 years (1981). In Southeast City, the study population had an average age of 71 years and a range of 55 to 83 years (Wentowski 1981). The residents of Midwest public housing were found to have a mean age of 74.6 and a range of 65 to 88 years (Stephens and Bernstein 1984). The relatively low range and average age of the West Coast population is no doubt a function of the substantial number of retired military personnel in the sample. Otherwise, the mean ages of the groups studied were quite similar.

The comparison studies use many different ways of classifying their samples in terms of occupation. The Midtown SRO study simply subdivided the sample into white collar (13 percent) and blue collar (87 percent) (Cohen and Sokolovsky 1981). Eckert used a more complex classification scheme, subtly different from those used in the other studies: white collar (15 percent), clerical/sales (15 percent), blue collar (60 percent), and military (10 percent) (1983). The Bowery Lunch Program study reported white collar (23 percent) and blue collar (77 percent). The Ridge County sample was fundamentally different. Over 70 percent of the men were farmers and most of the women reported that they were housewives. About ten percent were non-farmers.

The Midtown SRO (Cohen and Sokolovsky 1981:99) study classified alters as hotel contacts, outside nonkin contacts, and kin contacts. Almost half of all alters were hotel residents, and a third were outside nonkin contacts. Kin made up somewhat over a fifth of the relationships. A similar classification was used by Eckert (1983) in the West Coast SRO study: hotel, outside hotel and kin. Kin relationships made up 44 percent of ties, hotel residents 37 percent, and 19 percent were outside the hotel/ neighborhood. The Bowery men's networks consist of 36 percent hotel links, 28 percent outside kin, and 36 percent outside non-kin. The Southeastern City study classification scheme was derived from domain analysis technique (Spradley 1979; Frake 1964); Wentowski (1981) devised a schematic that divided "kinds of helpers" into kin and nonkin (1981). The non-kin were divided into friends and neighbors, and kin included those related "by blood" and "by marriage." The actual composition of these categories was not given. The Midwest public housing study classified relationships into the following categories: "residents of the housing facility" (35 percent), "family members" (44 percent), and "nonresident friends and associates" (20 percent) (Stephens and Bernstein 1984).

Only one of the studies reported importance of ties. The study of Bowery men reported that 32 percent of the network links were rated "very important" (Sokolovsky and Cohen 1978). The Midtown SRO study was the only one to record duration of links. In-hotel links had an average duration of seven years and outside-hotel ties had existed for an average of fifteen years. All the studies reported the incidence of kin in the network: 22 percent for the Midtown SRO study (Cohen and Sokolovsky 1981), 44 percent for the West Coast SRO study (Eckert 1983), 28 percent for the Bowery study (Sokolovsky and Cohen 1978), and 48 percent for the The Midwest public housing study (Stephens and Bernstein 1984).

Very important to our argument are the differences between the structures of the situations within which they live. First, all the panel studies were done in urban environments. Second, all the populations are in some way economically marginal, ranging from SRO hotel residents to subsidized housing residents.

None of the studies produced data on exchange equivalent to that gathered in Ridge County, although Stephens and Bernstein did refer to this dimension, attending to "advice" as a resource. In this study, advice is subsumed under general interaction. They did not deal with goods exchange, but did record "aid with meals." In their study, as in this one, food-related exchanges scored the highest after conversation and advice. Ste-

Table 9. Networks in the Comparison Panel

	Mean Size	Range
Ridge County	24.9	3-105
Bowery men	7.5	0-26
Midtown SRO	5.5	0-21
Midwest public housing	5.3	2-10
West Coast SRO	4.3	Not Reported

phens and Bernstein did not consider exchange complexity as such, but they did discover a significant association between "intimate conversation" and the exchange of more resources (1984:146). This mirrors the finding concerning the complexity of relationships with best friends. They reported that exchanges between residents in the public housing complex tended to be "evenly distributed"; in much the same way, there was symmetry in exchange between neighbors in Ridge County.

For our purposes, the important comparison is that of network size, presented here as a kind of dependent variable. The differences between the Ridge County sample and those of the comparison panel is large (see Table 9). It is clear that these studies are as closely related as one might expect for separate studies that are part of the same conception. Of course different operationalizations have large effects on the outcomes. The Midtown SRO study used the Network Analysis Profile, based on six fields of interaction. The network size variable is based on the three fields of interaction in what Cohen and Sokolovsky termed the "personal order," which in effect, excluded social service personnel and hotel staff. This exclusion makes the measurement logically different from that used in the Ridge County study but in a sense helps to control environmental differences. The Midtown study made use of a minimal frequency of interaction requirement that was less restrictive than that used in this study. The West Coast SRO study also used the "profile" technique, modified to add the idea of subjective "closeness" to interaction field listing criteria. The selection of fields for inclusion in the "personal zone" was similar to that used in the Midtown study. The Midwest public housing study made use of the "Support Network Inventory," which is conceptually similar to the network profile technique in that its primary listing criterion seems to be based on "resource exchange" truncated by a "field of interaction" approach. In identifying conversation as a resource, the Support Network Inventory resembles the Kentucky Exchange Network Inventory used in this study. Minimal frequency for listing was six months, a much less restrictive frequency criterion than was used in Ridge County. These differences in data collection may have reduced the differences in network size and range, and employing the same technique might have increased the differences. I used the profile technique with a few Ridge Countians experimentally and found that it produced larger networks.

If we assume comparability of these measures with the findings in Ridge County and take network size as a manifestation of the extent to which an individual is socially integrated or engaged, it is clear that the old people of Ridge County are the most socially integrated or engaged of all the elderly populations studied.[1] In this framework we are dealing with the local effects of the political economy. Choice structures behavior within the range allowed by local structural manifestations of the political economy, or the way economic reproduction, production, exchange and consumption are organized (Harris 1979:53). Choice is reciprocal: old people choose to interact, and others choose to interact with them. If we assume comparability of data, we need to interpret the differences between the communities, which seem immense, especially considered in terms of the network size norm of 25 developed by E. Mansell Pattison. If we allow ourselves to think of community structure as an independent variable, its effect on network size is of greater magnitude than any of the variables considered in the Ridge County study. It is even possible to conclude that the effect of aging itself is trivial compared to the effect of community structure. It seems that these different communities reflect different effects of the operation of changes occurring in Ridge County.

The economic process has changed the pattern of social re-

1. Aspects of the measurement are consistent and inconsistent with using these data comparatively. My ensuing contentions are based on the general notion that the people living in these other circumstances are significantly more isolated than people in Ridge County.

lationships in the different communities by separating production from consumption at the level of the household. It is a change associated with concentration of capital and specialization of production. People have less and less control over the means by which valuable things are produced, as production factors such as energy become delocalized. The factors that affect their lives are more and more influenced by the marketplace. Market decisions externalize the costs of production or shift them to someone else, away from the unit of production. This transition has many effects. For our consideration of the social lives of older people, two of the most important are the separation of the old and the young and reduction in neighborly economic cooperation. Complex forces based on market or government decisions stratify people according to age.

Market efficiencies are associated with grouping certain kinds of people. The populations of the comparison studies all manifest a high degree of age segregation. Historical analysis of Ridge County shows increasing age segregation from a past in which the old had a role in the household economy. They did what they could do, and the household economy internalized the cost of the inefficiency of their labor.

As the local economy becomes transformed, economic cooperation between neighbors and even household members becomes increasingly less feasible and therefore less frequent. The lack of these relationships leaves the old without identity in the exchange networks of the community. In places like Ridge County, as I have noted, the meanings associated with the relationships of exchange are very enduring. Others feel residual obligation for a long time. Further, these obligations generalize from family to family and between generations.

The norm of reciprocity is a foundation, and the diffuse reciprocities become generalized in both time and social space. This pattern is important because older people need to carry these relationship through time and to have other people assume the obligations to them of people who have died. One mechanism for diffusing obligation is the church, which has demonstrated importance as a place for groups of related people to get to know each other. Relationships at church are, to a large extent, family to family. Families see families together at church, and families tend to be dealt with as units. There is substantial motivation to have all members of a family saved so that they can be together forever. Family members, even those in other places, are mentioned in prayer lists. Many church members are seen in the context of multigenerational family groups. Intergenerational familial relationships are recognized and reinforced. In addition, intergenerational aid and assistance is modeled at church, mainly in the form of social interaction; the financial aid given is small. Church also serves as an efficient clearinghouse for information about the health and condition of older people, thus keeping even the isolated in public awareness. The circumstances of the political economy are tempered by a moral economy, which reduces the significance of wealth differences while it encourages people to care for each other.

Pervasive familiarity is, of course, facilitated by network density, the effects of which were recognized by Elizabeth Bott in her classic study of networks and families in London. "When many people a person knows interact with one another," she wrote, "that is when the person's social network is close-knit [that is, dense], and they exert consistent informal pressure on one another to conform to the norms, to keep in touch with one another, and, if need be, to help one another" (1964:60). The processes of change at work in Ridge County suggest that "new" old people will be increasingly isolated in the future because of limited formation of reciprocal relationships with neighbors and kin and the reduction in density of social ties.

This research is a reflection on the essential problem of social aging—that the old tend to become strangers in their own community (Beauvoir 1972, Gutmann 1980, Dowd 1986). The parent-child relationship is conditioned by a lifelong memory the child has of the parent's strength. As D. Guttmann asserts, the child "does not see in the parent a useless, ugly old person, Rather he still relates to the vigorous, sustaining parent that he once knew, as well as the weak person immediately before him" (1977:315). Parent-child familiarity is the archetype for other old-young relationships in society, but we must ask under what circumstances old people maintain their familiarity within a community. Reciprocity, generalized by community institutions such as the church, keeps old people from becoming strangers. It is the basis of social comprehension (Beauvoir 1972:216-22). In the absence of social comprehension, the person is a stranger.

This type of knowing is achieved through reciprocity to the extent that reciprocity incorporates others into our deliberative actions. Incorporation brings recognition of the goals of others as one works to achieve one's own goals. As Simone de Beauvoir writes, "In this relationship each steals one aspect of the real from the other and thereby shows him his boundaries" (1972:217). People become strangers when they exist beyond the time binding of reciprocal exchange, and being a stranger is fraught with risk. As Dowd says, "Once their connection with the past is severed, . . . the aged stranger arouses not deference but fear and loathing" (Dowd 1986:180, Guttman 1980).

The effects of reciprocity are coupled with the influences of cultural institutions like the church, which help to keep people from becoming "perfect strangers." D. Guttman has argued that it is a characteristic of what he calls "traditional society" that "the subjective tonus of 'we-ness' is extended to those individuals, of any age, who live according to the group consensus" (1980:441). We-ness is manifested in the context of Ridge County. Without the binding to the past and present, people are transformed from resources to waste by decisions beyond their control, and through these mechanisms old people become isolated. While these forces have much less effect in communities like Ridge County, they are apparent to those who have lived life in the old way.

While it is tempting to attribute the differences between Ridge County and the other areas studied to the contrast between rural and urban residence, to do so is to mask the real cause. As Goldschmidt so ably demonstrated in his comparison of three California farming communities, it is the relationship between people and economic production that structures social life (1947). In agricultural communities in which farming resources are concentrated—that is, owned by large-scale corporate interests—community social relationships become more stratified and less rich and supportive. Concentration of wealth destroys the intimate fabric of community life by making economic collaboration between households impossible. Work sharing works best between economic and social equals. Large farmers "share work" with small farmers by hiring them or making them tenants. These collaborations in inequality are carried out on the basis of the reciprocities of the marketplace. Labor is sold, provided for a fee. The paying of the fee to a large extent severs the binding with time and prevents the growth of diffuse obligations. W.P. Archibald's arguments concerning alienation provide a useful extension of the cases we are considering (1976). In a review article he considers the mechanisms by which persons of different class, status, or power avoid each other, how their relationships become narrow, and how relationships of this type tend be hostile.

Wendell Berry, too, has much to say that is pertinent to this discussion (1977:39-48). He interprets and describes the effects of this ecological transformation on the relationship between communities and the land (1977). Berry speaks of the revolutionary transformation of society in its relationship with agricultural production from that in which nurturance is the norm to a norm of exploitation. Exploitation is consistent with impermanence, ecological, social, and cognitive. The relatively diverse family-based agricultural production system of Ridge County still to a large extent follows Berry's conception of nurturance, as does Henry County, Kentucky, Berry's home. In such communities farming is done by families, farms are generally small; much of the household's food is produced on the farm and in a substantial garden; and a wide variety of commodities is produced, including livestock. Most labor is provided by the farmer and his family, and farming is still recognized as a skilled craft.

Berry argues that a special kind of caring relationship emerges under these conditions. As he says, "The nurturer serves land, household, community, place." (1977:8) Articulation with place is symptomatic of the nurturance of which Berry speaks. Here I have spoken of social articulation; Berry speaks primarily of environmental articulation. In Ridge County I have found a rich association between people; Berry finds this kind of association with place. Berry argues that "old associations" prepare human beings to care for the land. Nurturance requires and is expressed in permanence of relationship with place, people, and culture. Impermanence is consistent with careless and exploitative use of place, people, and culture. Old associations with people prepare us to care for each other.

It is apparent that more field research on aspects of social organization and structure would be useful. There are few comprehensive, community-based studies of social organization. To facilitate the examination of social networks, a standard data-collection technique would be more than useful. The Kentucky Exchange Network Inventory has certain advantages, most noteworthy of which is its apparently high level of transferability. The development of standard measures of social relationship needs to emphasize direct measurement, for the use of proxy measures reduces the potential for comparative analysis. The perspective needs to be naturalistic and verifiable through direct observation. Accurate and unbiased understanding of the position of older people in society is not possible without considering them as both sources and recipients of exchange. All humans give and receive. The effects of their giving are only now being understood (Stroller 1983, 1985a, 1985b). Thorough review of the literature on these aspects of the social life of old people will probably reveal a far larger number of studies that place emphasis on the old person as recipient rather than as reciprocal exchanger. Examining social relationships of older people without considering them as sources produces a distorted understanding of their social relationships, while it prevents public understanding of the contributions older people make to community life. Social science is valuable to the extent that it contributes to intelligent and effective policy and socially useful programs. It may be, however, that the social science of aging is fundamentally biased by these concerns. The underlying ideology appears to be appropriate to the furtherance of the goals of social service providers as agents of the power holders.

Also needed but subject to technical data-collection problems are naturalistic field studies of the processes of individual choice in reference to social organization. There are many studies of the psychological effect of choice and some studies of the social outcomes of individual choice, but there are virtually no naturalistic studies of individual processes of social organizational choice with attention to anticipation and adaptation. The significance of this approach for understanding cultural processes is immense (Barth 1967).

There needs to be an increased emphasis on studying social structure and organization in general. One can only agree with Mary Wylie's assessment that what is called social gerontology emphasizes the individual psychological dimension, while it invests little in understanding social structure at the community level or the nature of historical processes. Individuals exist in communities. Communities consist of structures of potential choices. Community structures are the products of complex, historic macro-processes. Individual life is expressed through choice. The choices of individuals influence the nature of the structures.

Appendix: Network Profile Instructions and Schedule

Instructions: This interview should be carried out in relative privacy, that is, other household members should not assist in providing information. The preferred place for the interview is the subject's home. Interviews should not be carried out at any other place for social interaction, such as church, school, or any mass data gathering event like a health fair. You are encouraged to engage the subject in any other discussion as you are moved. Be sure to record any of this additional data. *Do not rush the task.* The investigator wants quality data and comfortable interviewers. After completing a form make sure that all sheets are paper clipped together or stapled and that ID numbers are *recorded on each slip*. You will be debriefed concerning each form you collected. This will occur frequently during the week.

You will be required to keep a journal in which, following your interview you will record date, time, duration of interview, responsiveness of subject, problems of cooperation, and the like. Incidental comments on social organization will be most welcome.

The task which you will present to the subejcts will involve listing their first-order network zone constituents. There is a set of listing criteria provided below. It is not necessary to read this to the subject but you should be thoroughly familiar with the criteria so as to adjudicate any ambiguities.

Listing Criteria

1. The frame of reference is the person's typical experience, not a specific period of time. The general question is "Who do you usually see," not "Who did you see this month."

2. For an alter to be listed the subject must be able to report the alter's first and last name. Nicknames are acceptable. Family names

(surnames) alone are unacceptable, as are teknonyms. Thus "that Smith girl" or "Joe Adam's boy" are *not* to be listed.

3. A person should be listed only if he or she has actually engaged in conversation with the subject that is greater than minimal spoken greetings. Conversation must be interactive. That is, a preacher's sermon to the subject should not cause the persons preacher to be listed, but the conversation after church will if it goes beyond, "Hello. How are you? . . . I am fine." The minimal interaction will have at least three beats to it, that is the simple exchange of greetings is an inadequate justification for listing. Telephone interaction is all right.

4. It is assumed that people will overreport those they like and think well of. They will underreport those they don't like. You may remind them that affection is not what we are attempting to measure.

5. Communication by letters doesn't count, although it does represent information we are interested in. The data collection form starts with some rather straightforward questions, such as date of birth and name. You will already have the person's ID number, and this data, taken together, will allow you to match the data with the sample list and other aspects of the data base.

Name: Obtain as full a name as possible. Get maiden name of all females. Put maiden name in parentheses.

Driver's License: Must have a currently valid driver's license.

Own Car: Must be running.

Phone: Must have a phone within the house that is operating. If they say they use their neighbor's phone code it no phone, but note it marginally.

Distance to nearest house: This should be done by observation. There are three categories. 1) Another house is within 100 feet or less, this is for city lots. 2) Next house is visible but is more than 100 feet away. 3) Isolated house, no neighbors visible from point of entry into the house.

Level of physical mobility: The need here is to develop an understanding of any gross restrictions on mobility.

Retirement: Take what ever descriptive term is provided by the informant.

Listing: Part of the research task is to produce a list of people's names. The procedure requires that the subject be able to read the list. Therefore, you should write the list carefully with a good pen.

Network Profile Schedule

The questions and probes listed here are to be used with a special data recording form. There are special instructions for the use of this form and schedule. All the items which are in UPPER CASE are to be read to the research subject.

WE ARE TRYING TO FIND OUT MORE ABOUT PEOPLE'S SOCIAL RE-LATIONSHIPS AS THEY GROW OLDER. YOU COULD HELP US VERY MUCH BY TELLING ME THE NAMES OF ALL THE PEOPLE YOU USUALLY TALK TO. THESE PEOPLE CAN BE NEIGHBORS, FRIENDS, RELATIVES, PEOPLE YOU WORK WITH, FELLOW MEMBERS OF ORGANIZATIONS OR ANY-BODY ELSE YOU TALK TO. WE WILL ASK YOU A FEW QUESTIONS ABOUT THESE PEOPLE.

(proceed without hesitation)

FIRST TELL ME THE NAMES OF THE PEOPLE YOU ARE LIKELY TO TALK TO EVERY DAY, EITHER FACE-TO-FACE OR BY PHONE. I WILL PUT THEIR NAMES ON THIS LIST.

(list on form provided)

NOW TELL ME THE NAMES OF THE PEOPLE YOU TALK TO MORE THAN ONCE A WEEK BUT NOT EVERY DAY.

(list on form provided)

NOW TELL ME THE NAMES OF THE PEOPLE YOU TALK TO AT LEAST ONCE A WEEK.

(list on form provided)

NOW TELL ME THE NAMES OF THE PEOPLE YOU TALK TO AT LEAST ONCE A MONTH.

(list on form provided)

HERE IS THE LIST OF PEOPLE, CAN YOU THINK OF ANY ADDITIONS?

(list on form provided)

ARE THERE ANY RELATIVES OR FRIENDS WHO AREN'T ON THIS LIST BECAUSE YOU SEE THEM ONLY A FEW TIMES A YEAR?

Instructions to interviewer: At this point you will have a list of names recorded on the form. You will ask the subject a short series of questions about each person on the list.

Column 17: This column is to be used for coding the frequency category. The codes used are 1 is daily, 2 is more than once a week but not daily, 3 is once a week, 4 is once a month. These should be recorded as you are are recording names.

Column 18: Sex of network person? _____ M = 1 F = 2

Column 19: Do you know how old this person is? _____ 1 = 0-19, 2 = 20 . . . 9 = 90+; 0 = missing. This will be coded as older is 1, younger is 2, and same is 3.

Ask the person being interviewed questions appropriate to the fol-lowing coding instructions. With some individuals you might want to let them check the appropriate boxes.

Column 20: CHECK ALL THOSE PEOPLE WHO DO NOT LIVE IN THE COUNTY.

Column 21: CHECK ALL THOSE PEOPLE YOU WOULD CONSIDER RELATIVES.

Column 22: CHECK ALL THOSE PEOPLE YOU WORK WITH (CO-WORKERS).

Column 23: CHECK ALL YOUR FELLOW MEMBERS OF ORGANIZATIONS.

Column 24: CHECK ALL THOSE PEOPLE WHOM YOU THINK OF AS NEIGHBORS.

Column 25: CHECK ALL THOSE PERSONS YOU WOULD CONSIDER FRIENDS.

Column 26: CHECK THAT PERSON WHOM YOU WOULD CONSIDER YOUR BEST FRIEND.

Column 27: CHECK ALL THOSE PERSONS YOU HAVE TO YOUR HOUSE TO EAT.

Column 28: CHECK ALL THOSE PERSONS YOU HAVE MEALS WITH AT THEIR HOUSE.

Column 29: CHECK ALL THOSE PERSONS YOU GIVE GIFTS OF FOOD OR DRINK TO.

Column 30: CHECK ALL THOSE PERSONS WHO GIVE GIFTS OF FOOD OR DRINK TO YOU.

Column 31: CHECK ALL THOSE PERSONS YOU GIVE OTHER GIFTS TO.

Column 32: CHECK ALL THOSE PERSONS WHO GIVE GIFTS TO YOU.

Column 33: CHECK ALL THOSE PERSONS YOU HELP WHEN THEY ARE SICK.

Column 34: CHECK ALL THOSE PERSONS WHO HELP YOU WHEN YOU ARE SICK.

Column 35: CHECK ALL THOSE PERSONS WHO YOU HIRE TO DO WORK FOR YOU.

Column 36: CHECK ALL THOSE PERSONS WHO HIRE YOU TO WORK FOR THEM.

Column 37: CHECK ALL THOSE PERSONS YOU WORK FOR FOR FREE.

Column 38: CHECK ALL THOSE PERSONS WHO WORK FOR YOU FOR FREE.

Column 39: CHECK ALL THOSE PERSONS YOU SHOP FOR.

Column 40: CHECK ALL THOSE PERSONS WHO SHOP FOR YOU.

Column 41: CHECK ALL THOSE PERSONS YOU BORROW MONEY FROM.

Column 42: CHECK ALL THOSE PERSONS YOU LEND MONEY TO.

Column 43: CHECK ALL THOSE PERSONS THAT YOU BORROW THINGS FROM.

Column 44: CHECK ALL THOSE PEOPLE YOU LEND THINGS TO.

Column 45: Instructions: Show the research subject the stairsteps sheet.

WE CAN SAY THAT SOME RELATIONSHIPS ARE MORE IMPORTANT THAN OTHERS. THINKING OF THESE STAIRSTEPS, TELL ME HOW IMPORTANT IS THE RELATIONSHIP YOU HAVE WITH THIS PERSON. REMEMBER, FIVE MEANS THE MOST IMPORTANT AND ONE MEANS THE LEAST IMPORTANT. YOU CAN USE THE OTHER NUMBERS TO SHOW THE LEVELS OF IMPORTANCE WHICH ARE IN-BETWEEN.

Column 46: IN THE LAST SQUARE WRITE DOWN THE NUMBER OF YEARS YOU HAVE KNOWN THIS PERSON. IF YOU HAVE KNOWN THIS PERSON LESS THAN A YEAR, WRITE ONE.

References Cited

Aday, R. H., and L. A. Miles. 1982. Long-Term Impacts of Rural Migration of the Elderly: Implications for Research. *Gerontologist* 22:331-36.

Alford, R. 1976. *Health Care Politics*. Chicago: Univ. of Chicago Press.

Allen, James Lane. 1889. County Court Day in Kentucky. *Harper's Magazine* 79:383-99.

Archibald, W. P. 1976. Face-to-Face: The Alienating Effects of Class, State, and Power Divisions. *American Sociological Review* 41:819-37.

Arcury, Thomas A. 1983. Household Structure and Economic Change in a Rural Community, 1900 to 1980. Ph.D. diss., Univ. of Kentucky.

————. 1984. Household Composition and Economic Change in a Rural Community, 1900-1980: Testing Two Models. *American Ethnologist* 11:677-98.

————. 1986. Rural Elderly Household Life-Course Transitions, 1900 and 1980 Compared. *Journal of Family History* 11:55-76.

Arensberg, Conrad M. and Solon T. Kimball. 1968. *Family and Community in Ireland*. 2d edition. Cambridge: Harvard Univ. Press.

Atchley, R.C. 1971. Disengagement among Professors. *Journal of Gerontology* 26(4):476-80.

Atchley, R.C., and S.J. Miller. 1979. Housing and Households of the Rural Aged. In *Environmental Context of Aging: Lifestyles, Environmental Quality, and Living Arrangements*. 62-79. New York: Garland STPM Press.

Auerbach, A.J. 1976. The Elderly in Rural and Urban Areas. In *Social Work in Rural Communities*, edited by L.H. Ginsberg, 99-107. New York: Council on Social Work Education.

Axton, W.F. 1975. *Tobacco and Kentucky*. Lexington: Univ. Press of Kentucky.

Banfield, Edward C. 1958. *The Moral Basis of a Backward Society*. Glencoe, Ill.: Free Press.

References Cited 169

Barlett, Peggy, ed. 1980. *Agricultural Decision Making: Anthropological Contributions to Rural Development.* New York: Academic Press.

Barnes, J.A. 1954. Class and Committees in a Norwegian Parish Island. *Human Relations* 7:39-58.

————. 1969. Graph Theory and Social Network: A Technical Comment on Connectedness and Connectivity. *Sociology* 3:215-32.

————. 1972. *Social Networks.* An Addison-Wesley Module in Anthropology, Module 26. Reading, Mass.: Addison-Wesley.

Barth, Frederick. 1967. On the Study of Social Change. *American Anthropologist* 69(6):661-69.

Beale, C.L. 1975. *The Revival of Population Growth in Nonmetropolitan America.* Washington, D.C.: United States Department of Agriculture, Economic Research Service.

Beale, C.L. and G.V. Fuguitt. 1978. The New Pattern of Nonmetropolitan Population Change. In *Social Demography,* edited by K.E. Taeuber, L.L. Bumpass and J.A. Sweet, 157-177. New York: Academic Press.

Beauvoir, Simone de. 1972. *The Coming of Age.* New York: Putnam and Sons.

Bengston, Vern L. 1973. *The Social Psychology of Aging.* Indianapolis: Bobbs-Merrill.

————. 1979. Ethnicity and Aging: Problems and Issues in Current Social Science Inquiry. In *Ethnicity and Aging,* edited by D.E. Gelfand and A.J. Kutzik, 9-31. New York: Springer.

Bengston, Vern L. and James J. Dowd. 1980. Sociological Functionalism, Exchange Theory and Life Cycle Analysis: A Call for More Explicit Theoretical Bridges. *International Journal of Aging and Human Development* 12(1):55-73.

Bennett, John W. 1969. *Northern Plainsmen.* Arlington Heights, Ill.:AHR.

————. 1976. *The Ecological Transition: Cultural Anthropology and Human Adaptation.* New York: Pergamon.

Berkowitz, S.D. 1982. *An Introduction to Structural Analysis: The Network Approach to Social Research.* Toronto: Butterworths.

Bernard, H. Russell, and Peter D. Killworth. 1973. On the Social Structure of an Oceangoing Research Vessel and Other Important Things. *Social Science Research* 2:145-84.

————. 1977. Informant Accuracy in Social Network Data, II. *Human Communication Research.* 4:3-18.

Bernard, H. Russell, Peter D. Killworth, and Lee Sailer. 1980. Informant Accuracy in Social Network Data IV: A Comparison of Clique-Level Structure in Behavioral and Cognitive Network Data. *Social Networks* 2:191-218.

————. 1981. A Review of Informant Accuracy in Social Network Data.

In *Modelle fur Ausbreitungsprozesse in Socialen Strukturen*, edited by H.J. Hummell and W. Sodeur, 153-86. Duisberg: Sozialwissenshaftlichen Kooperative.

―――. 1982. Informant Accuracy in Social Network Data, V: An Experimental Attempt to Predict Actual Communication from Recall Data. *Social Science Research* 11:30-66.

Berry, Wendell. 1970. The Regional Motive. In *A Continuous Harmony: Essays Cultural and Agricultural*. New York: Harcourt, Brace, Jovanovich.

―――. 1974. *The Memory of Old Jack*. New York: Harcourt, Brace, Jovanovich.

―――. 1977. *The Unsettling of America: Culture and Agriculture*. San Francisco: Sierra Club Books.

Blau, Peter M. 1947. *Exchange and Power in Social Life*. New York: John Wiley and Sons.

Blau, Z.S. 1973. *Old Age in a Changing Society*. New York: New Viewpoints.

Boissevain, J. 1968. The Place on Non-groups in the Social Sciences. *Man*. n.s. 3:269-75.

―――. 1974. *Friends of Friends*. Oxford: Basil Blackwell.

Bott, Elizabeth. 1964. *Family and Social Network: Roles, Norms and External Relationships in Ordinary Urban Families*. London: Tavistock.

―――. 1971. *Family and Social Network: Roles, Norms and External Relationships in Ordinary Urban Families*. 2d edition. London: Tavistock.

Bryant, F. Carlene. 1981. *We're All Kin: A Cultural Study of a Mountain Neighborhood*. Knoxville: University of Tennessee Press.

Burt, R.S. and W.M. Bittner. 1981. A Note on Inferences Regarding Network Subgroups. *Social Networks* 3:71-83.

Butler, R.N. 1963. The Life Review: An Interpretation of Reminiscences in the Aged. *Psychiatry* 26: 65-76.

Cain, L.D., Jr. 1959. The Sociology of Aging: A Trend Report and Biography. *Current Sociology* 8:57-133, 159.

Campbell, Donald T. 1966. Variation and Selective-Retention in Sociocultural Evolution. In *Social Change in Developing Areas: A Reinterpretation of Evolutionary Theory*, edited by H. Barringer, G. Blanksten, and R. Mack, 19-49. Cambridge, Mass.:Schenkman Cantril, H. 1965. *The Pattern of Human Concerns*. New Jersey: Rutgers Univ. Press.

Caplow, T. 1955. The Definition and Measurement of Ambiences. *Social Forces* 9:28-33.

Clark, M. Margaret and Barbara Anderson. 1967. *Culture and Aging: An Anthropological Study of Older Americans*. Springfield, Ill.: Charles C. Thomas.

Clark, Thomas D. 1979. Statement on File at Kentucky Rivers Coalition Office, Lexington.

Cohen, Carl I. and Jay Sokolovsky. 1981. A Reassessment of the Sociability of Long-Term Skid Row Residents: A Social Network Approach. *Social Networks* 3:93-105.

Cottrell, F. 1971. *Transportation of Older People in a Rural Community*. Oxford, Ohio: Scripps Foundation.

———. 1975. Transportation of the Rural Aged. in *Rural Environments and Aging*, edited by R. Atchley, 187-215. Washington, D.C.: Gerontology Society of America.

Coward, Raymond T. 1979. Planning Community Services for the Elderly: Implications from Research. *Gerontologist* 19: 275-282.

Coward, Raymond T. and Gary R. Lee, eds. 1985. *The Elderly in Rural Society: Every Fourth Elder*. Springer Series on Adulthood and Aging. New York: Springer.

Cowgill, Donald and Lowell Holmes. 1972. *Aging and Modernization*. New York: Appleton—Century—Crofts.

Craven, Paul, and Barry Wellman. 1973. The Network City. *Sociological Inquiry* 3-4:57-88.

Cumming, Elaine M. 1964. New Thoughts on the Theory of Disengagement. In *New Thoughts on Old Age* edited by R. Kastenbaum, 3-6. New York: Springer.

———. 1976. *Further Thoughts on the Theory of Disengagement*. In Aging in America: Readings in Social Gerontology, edited by C.S. Kart and B. Manard, 19-41. New York: Alfred.

Cumming, Elaine, L.R. Dean, D.S. Newell and J. McCaffrey. 1960. Disengagement—A Tentative Theory of Aging. *Sociometry* 23(1):25-35.

Cumming, Elaine, and W.E. Henry. 1961. *Growing Old: The Process of Disengagement*. New York: Basic Books.

Cutler, S.J. 1975. Transportation and Change in Life Satisfaction. *Gerontologist* 15:155-59.

De Laguna, Grace. 1960. The Lebenswelt and the Cultural World.

———. *Journal of Philosophy* 57(25):777-91.

DeWalt, Billie R. and Pertti J. Pelto. 1985. *Micro and Macro Levels of Analysis in Anthropology: Issues in Theory and Method*. Boulder, Colo.: Westview Press.

Donnenwerth, G.V., R. Guy, and M.J. Norvell. 1978. Life Satisfaction among Older Persons: Rural-Urban and Racial Comparisons. *Social Service Quarterly* 59:578-83.

Doreian, P. 1974. On the Connectivity of Social Networks. *Journal of Mathematical Sociology* 3:245-58

Dowd, James J. 1975. Aging as Exchange: A Preface to Theory. *Journal of Gerontology* 30(5):584-94.

———. 1980. Stratification among the Aged. Monterey, Calif.: Brooks/Cole.

———. 1986. The Old Person as Stranger. In *Later Life, The Social Psy-*

172 References Cited

chology of Aging, edited by Victor W. Marshall, 147-189. Beverly Hills, Calif.: Sage.

Downing, J. 1957. Factors Affecting the Selective Use of a Social Club for the Aged. *Journal of Gerontology* 12:81-84.

Eckert, J. Kevin. 1980. *The Unseen Elderly, A Study of Marginally Subsistent Hotel Dwellers*. San Diego, Calif.: Campanile Press, San Diego State.

————. 1983. Dislocation and Relocation of the Urban Elderly: Social Networks as Mediators of Relocation Stress. *Human Organization* 42(1):39-45.

Eggan, F. 1954. Social Anthropology and the Method of the Controlled Comparison. *American Anthropologist* 56:743-63.

Elder, Glen H., Jr. 1974. *Children of the Great Depression*. Chicago: Univ. of Chicago Press.

————. 1987. Families and Lives: Some Developments in Life-Course Studies. *Journal of Family History* 12:179-99.

Epstein, A. L. 1969. The Network and Urban Social Organization. In *Social Networks in Urban Situations*, edited by J. Clyde Mitchell, 77-127. Manchester: Manchester Univ. Press.

Estes, Carroll L. 1979. Toward a Sociology of Political Gerontology. *Sociological Symposium* 26:1-27.

————. 1979b. *The Aging Enterprise: A Critical Examination of Social Policies and Services for the Aged*. San Francisco: Jossey-Bass.

Estes, Carroll L., et al. 1984. *Political Economy, Health, and Aging*. New York: Little, Brown.

Estes, C.L. and H.E. Freeman. 1976. Strategies of Design and Research for Intervention. In *Handbook of Aging and the Social Sciences*, edited by R.H. Binstock and E. Shanas, 536-60. New York: D. Van Nostrand.

Faragher, John Mack. 1985. Open-Country Community: Sugar Creek, Illinois, 1820-1950. In *The Countryside in the Age of Capitalist Transformation: Essays in the Social History of Rural America*, edited by Steven Hahn and Jonathan Prude, 233-58. Chapel Hill: Univ. of North Carolina Press.

Firth, Raymond. 1961. *Elements of Social Organization*. 3d edition (orig. 1951). Boston: Beacon Press.

Fischer, Claude S. 1982. What Do We Mean by 'Friend'? An Inductive Study. *Social Network* 3:287-306.

Fischer, David Hackett. 1977. *Growing Old in America*. New York: Oxford Univ. Press.

Fisher, James and Ronald Mitchelson. 1981. Forces of Change in the American Settlement Pattern. *Geographical Review* 71:298-310.

Fortes, Meyer. 1949. *The Web of Kinship among the Tallensi*. London: Oxford Univ. Press.

Frake, Charles O. 1962. The Ethnographic Study of Cognitive Systems. In *Anthropology and Human Behavior*, edited by Thomas Gladwin and

William C. Sturtevant, 72-85. Washington, D.C.: Anthropological Society of Washington.

———. 1964. Notes on Queries in Ethnography. *American Anthropologist* 66:132-45.

Francis, Doris. 1984. *Will You Still Need Me, Will You Still Feed Me, When I'm 84?* Bloomington: Indiana Univ. Press.

Frankenberg, R.J. 1966. *Communities in Britain: Social Life in Town and Country*, Harmondsworth; Eng.:Penguin Books.

Freeman, Linton C., A. Kimball Romney and Sue C. Freeman. 1987. Cognitive Structure and Informant Accuracy. *American Anthropologist* 89(2):310-25.

Fry, Christine L. et al, eds. 1980. *Aging in Culture and Society*. New York: J.E. Bergin.

Fry, Christine L. and Jennie Keith. 1986. *New Methods for Old Age Research*. South Hadley, Mass.:Bergin and Garvey.

Fuguitt, G.V. and S.J. Tordella. 1980. Elderly Net Migration: The New Trend of Nonmetropolitan Population Change. *Research on Aging* 2:191-204.

Geertz, Clifford. 1973. *The Interpretation of Cultures*. New York:Basic Books.

Gluckman, Max. 1955. *The Judicial Process among the Barotse of Northern Rhodesia*. Manchester: Manchester Univ. Press for the Rhodes-Livingston Institute.

———. 1962. Les Rites de Passage. In *Essays in the Ritual of Social Relations*, edited by M. Gluckman, 1-52, Manchester: Manchester Univ. Press.

Goldschmidt, Walter R. 1947. *As You Sow*. New York: Harcourt, Brace.

Gouldner, A.W. 1960. The Norm of Reciprocity: A Preliminary Statement. *American Sociological Review* 25:161-178.

Graney, M.J. 1975. Happiness and Social Participation in Old Age. *Journal of Gerontology* 30:701-6.

Gubrium, Jaber. 1973. *The Myth of the Golden Years: A Socio-environmental Theory of Aging*. Springfield, Ill.: Charles C. Thomas.

Guttmann, D. 1977. The Cross-Cultural Perspective: Notes toward a Comparative Psychology of Aging. In *Handbook of the Psychology of Aging*, edited by J.E. Birren and K.W. Schaie, 302-321, New York: Van Nostrand, Reinhold.

———. 1980. Observation on Culture and Mental Health in Later Life. In *Handbook of Mental Health and Aging*, edited by J.E. Birren and R.B. Sloan, 429-447, Englewood Cliffs, N.J.: Prentice-Hall

Haber, Carole. 1983. *Beyond Sixty-five, The Dilemma of Old Age in America's Past*. Cambridge: Cambridge Univ. Press.

Habermas, Jurgen. 1971. *Knowledge and Human Interests*. Boston: Beacon.

Hage, Per, and Frank Harary. 1983. *Structural Models in Anthropology*. Cambridge: Cambridge Univ. Press.

Hahn, Steven. 1985. The "Unmaking" of the Southern Yeomanry: The Transformation of the Georgia Upcountry, 1860-1890. In *The Countryside in the Age of Capitalist Transformation: Essays in the Social History of Rural America*, edited by Steven Hahn and Jonathan Prude, 179-203. Chapel Hill: Univ. of North Carolina Press.

Harary, F., R.Z. Norman and D. Cartwright. 1965. *Graph Theory as a Mathematical Model in Social Sciences*. New York: John Wiley & Sons.

Harris, C.S. 1978. *Fact Book on Aging: A Profile of America's Older Population*. Washington, D.C.: National Council in the Aging.

Harris, Marvin. 1964. *The Nature of Cultural Things*. New York: Random House.

————. 1979. *Cultural Materialism, The Struggle for a Science of Culture*. New York: Vintage.

Havighurst, Robert J. 1963. Successful Aging. In *Processes of Aging*, edited by R. Williams, C. Tibbits, and W. Donohue, 299-311. New York: Atherton.

Havighurst, R.J. and R. Albrecht. 1953. *Older People*. New York: Longmans, Green.

Havighurst, Robert J., Bernice L. Neugarten, and Sheldon S. Tobin. 1968. Disengagement and Patterns of Aging. In *Middle Age and Aging*, edited by Bernice L. Neugarten, 161-172. Chicago: Univ. of Chicago Press.

Heckathorn, D. 1979. The Anatomy of Social Linkages. *Social Science Research* 8:222-52.

Hendricks, Jon, and C. Davis Hendricks. 1981. *Aging in Mass Society, Myths and Realities*. Cambridge, Mass.: Winthrop.

Henry, Jules. 1958. The Personal Community and its Invariant Properties. *American Anthropologist* 60:827-31.

Henry, W.E. 1965. Engagement and Disengagement: Toward a Theory of Adult Development. In *Contributions to the Psycho-Biology of Aging*, edited by Robert Kastenbaum, 19-35. New York: Springer.

Hochschild, Arlie R. 1975. Disengagement Theory: A Critique and Proposal. *American Sociological Review* 4:553-69.

————. 1976. Disengagement Theory: A Logical, Empirical, Phenomenological Critique. In *Time Roles and Self in Old Age*, edited by Jaber F. Gubrium, 53-87, New York: Human Sciences Press.

Homans, George C. 1941. *English Villagers of the Thirteenth Century*. Cambridge: Harvard Univ. Press.

Hynson, L.M. 1976. Rural-Urban Differences in Satisfaction among the Elderly. *Rural Sociology* 40:269-75.

Ireland, Robert M. 1972. *The County Courts in Antebellum Kentucky*. Lexington, Univ. Press of Kentucky.

———. 1976. *The County in Kentucky History*. Lexington: Univ. Press of Kentucky.

Jay, E.J. 1964. The Concepts of 'Field' and 'Network' in Anthropological Research. *Man* 177:137-39.

John, Robert. 1985. Service Needs and Support Networks of Elderly Native Americans: Family, Friends, and Social Service Agencies. In *Social Bonds in Later Life*, edited by Warren A. Peterson and Jill Quadagno, 229-247. Beverly Hills, Calif.:Sage.

Kapferer, B. 1969. Norms and the Manipulation of Relationships in a Work Context. In *Social Networks in Urban Situations*, edited by J. Clyde Mitchell, 181-244. Manchester Eng.: Manchester Univ. Press.

———. 1973. Social Network and Conjugal Role in Urban Zambia: Towards a Reformulation of the Bott Hypothesis. In *Network Analysis*, edited by J. Boissevain and J.C. Mitchell, The Hague:Mouton.

Katz, E. 1966. Social Participation and Social Structure. *Social Forces* 45:299-310.

Keith, Jennie. 1982. *Old People as People, Social and Cultural Influences on Aging and Old Age*. Boston: Little, Brown.

Killworth, Peter and H. Russell Bernard. 1974. Catij: A New Sociometric and Its Application to a Prison Living Unit. *Human Organization* 33(4):335-50.

———. 1976. Informant Accuracy in Social Network Data. *Human Organization* 35:269-86.

———. 1979. Informant Accuracy in Social Network Data, III. A Comparison of Triadic Structure in Behavioral and Cognitive Data. *Social Networks* 2:19-46.

Kim, Paul. 1981. The Low Income Rural Elderly: Under-served Victims of Public Inequity. In *Toward Mental Health of the Rural Elderly*, edited by P. Kim and Constance Wilson, 15-27. Washington, D.C.: Univ. Press of America.

Kim, Paul K., and Constance Wilson, eds. 1981. *Toward Mental Health of the Rural Elderly*. Washington, D.C.: Univ. Press of America.

Knoke, David, and James H. Kuklinski. 1982. Network Analysis. Sage Univ. Paper Series on Quantitative Applications in the Social Sciences, no. 28. Beverly Hills; Calif.: Sage.

Kovar, M.G. 1977. Health of the Elderly and the Use of Health Services. *Public Health Reports* 92:9-19.

Krout, John A. 1983. Knowledge and Use of Services by the Elderly: A Critical Review of the Literature. *International Journal of Aging and Human Development* 17:153-67.

———. 1986. *The Aged in Rural America*. Contributions to the Study of Aging, no. 5. New York: Greenwood Press.

Leach, Edmund. 1954. *Political Systems of Highland Burma; A Study of Kachin Social Structure*. Cambridge: Harvard Univ. Press.

Lee, G.R. and M.L. Lassey. 1980. Rural-Urban Differences among the Elderly: Economic, Social and Subjective Factors. *Journal of Social Issues* 36:62-74.

Lemon, Bruce W., Vern L. Bengtson, and James A. Peterson. 1972. An Exploration of the Activity Theory of Aging: Activity Types and Life Satisfaction among In-Movers to a Retirement Community. *Journal of Gerontology* 27:511-23.

Leveton, L., et al. 1979. Social Support and Well-being in Urban Elderly. Paper presented at Gerontological Society Meetings.

Levi-Strauss, Claude. 1949. *The Elementary Structures of Kinship*. Boston: Beacon Press.

Long, Larry, and Diana DeAre. 1982. Repopulating the Countryside: A 1980 Census Trend. *Science* 217:1111-16.

Lonsdale, Richard E. 1981. Industry's Role in Nonmetropolitan Development Policy. In *Population Redistribution in the Midwest*, edited by Curtis C. Roseman, Andrew J. Sofranko, and James D. Williams, 129-48. Ames, Iowa:North Central Regional Center for Rural Development, Iowa State University.

Lowenthal, M.F. 1968. Social Isolation and Mental Illness in Old Age. In *Middle Age and Aging*, edited by B. Neugarten, 220-234, Chicago: Univ. of Chicago Press.

Lowenthal, Marjorie F. and Betsy Robinson. 1976. Social Networks and Isolation. In *Handbook of Aging and the Social Sciences*, edited by R.H. Binstock and E. Shanas, 432-456. New York: Van Norstrand.

Maddox, G.L. 1963. Activity and Morale: A Longitudinal Study of Selected Elderly Subjects. *Social Forces* 42:195-204.

———. 1964. Disengagement Theory: A Critical Evaluation. *Gerontologist* 4(2):80-82.

———. 1968. Persistence of Life Style among the Elderly: A Longitudinal Study of Patterns of Social Activity in Relation to Life Satisfaction. In *Middle Age and Aging*, edited by B.L. Neugarten, 181-183, Chicago: Univ.of Chicago Press.

Mancini, Jay A., William Quinn, Miriam Aberg Gavigan, and Henrietta Franklin. 1980. Social Network Interaction among Older Adults: Implications for Life Satisfaction. *Human Relations* 33(8):543-54.

Marshall, Victor W. 1986. Dominant and Emerging Paradigms in the Social Psychology of Aging. In *Later Life, the Social Psychology of Aging*, edited by Victor W. Marshall, 9-31. Beverly Hills, Calif.:Sage.

Martin, Charles E. 1984. *Hollybush: Folk Building and Social Change in an Appalachian Community*. Knoxville: Univ. of Tennessee Press.

Mauss, Marcel. 1954. *The Gift*. New York: Free Press.

Mayer, A.C. 1966. The Significance of Quasi-Groups in the Study of Complex Societies. In *The Social Anthropology of Complex Societies*, edited by Michael Banton, 97-122. London: Tavistock.

Mayo, Selz C. 1950. Age Profiles of Social Participation in Rural Areas of Wake County, N.C. *Rural Sociology* 15:242-51.

Milgram, S. 1969. Interdisciplinary Thinking and the Small World Problem. In *Interdisciplinary Relationships in the Social Sciences*, edited by M. Sherif and C.W. Sherif. Chicago: Aldine.

Miller, G.A. 1956. The Magical Number Seven, Plus or Minus Two: Some Limits on Our Capacity for Processing Information. *Psychological Review* 63:81-97.

Mills, C. Wright. 1959. *The Sociological Imagination*. New York: Oxford Univ. Press.

Minkler, Meredith. 1984. Introduction to *Readings in the Political Economy of Aging*, edited by Minkler and Carroll L. Estes, 10-22. Policy, Politics, Health and Medicine Series, no. 60. Farmingdale, N.Y.: Baywood.

Minkler, Meredith, and Carroll L. Estes, eds. 1984. *Readings in the Political Economy of Aging*. Policy, Politics, Health and Medicine Series, no. 6. Farmingdale, N.Y.: Baywood.

Mitchell, J. Clyde. 1969. The Concept and Use of Social Networks. In *Social Networks in Urban Situations: Analyses of Personal Relationships in Central African Towns*, edited by J. Clyde Mitchell, Manchester Eng.: Manchester Univ. Press.

Montgomery, J.E., A.C. Stubbs, and S.S. Day. 1980. The Housing Environment of the Rural Elderly. *Gerontologist* 20:444-51.

Moon, M. 1977. *The Measurement of Economic Welfare: Its Application to the Aged Poor*. New York: Academic Press.

Murdock, George P., Clellan S. Ford, Alfred E. Hudson, Raymond Kennedy, Leo W. Simmons and John W. M. Whiting. 1971. *Outline of Cultural Materials*, 4th revised edition, 5th printing with modifications. New Haven, Conn.: Human Relations Area Files.

Myerhoff, Barbara. 1978. *Number our Days*. New York: Dutton.

Nelson, G. 1980. Social Services to the Urban and Rural Aged: The Experience of Area Agencies on Aging. *Gerontologist* 20(2):200-07.

Norman, Dennis K., J. Michael Murphy, Carol Gilligan, and Jyotsna Vasudev. 1982. Sex Differences and Interpersonal Relationships: A Cross-Sectional Sample in the U.S. and India. *International Journal of Aging and Human Development* 14(4):291-306.

Olson, Laura Katz. 1982. *The Political Economy of Aging, The State, Private Power, and Social Welfare*. New York: Columbia Univ. Press.

Ortner, Sherry B. 1973. On Key Symbols. *American Anthropologist* 75:1338-46.

Pattison, E. Mansell. 1977. A Theoretical-Empirical Base for Social Systems Therapy. In *Current Perspectives in Cultural Psychiatry*, edited by E. Foulkes, 217-53 New York: Spectrum.

———. n.d. *The Psychosocial Network Inventory*. Santa Ana, Calif.: Department of Mental Health, County of Orange.

Pattison, E. Mansell, D. Francisco and P. Wood. 1975. A Psychosocial Kinship Model for Family Therapy. *American Journal of Psychiatry* 132(12):1246-51.

Patton, C.V. 1975. Age Grouping and Travel in a Rural Area. *Rural Sociology* 40:55-63.

Pelto, Pertti and Gretel H. Pelto. 1978. *Anthropological Research: The Structure of Inquiry.* 2d edition. New York: Cambridge Univ. Press.

Phillips, B.S. 1957. A Role Theory Approach to Adjustment in Old Age. *American Sociological Review* 22(2):212-27.

Pihlblad, C.T. and D.L. Adams. 1972. Widowhood, Social Participation and Life Satisfaction. *Aging and Human Development* 3:323-30.

Pike, Kenneth L. 1954. *Language in Relation to a Unified Theory of the Structure of Human Behavior.* Glendale, Calif.: Summer Institute of Linguistics.

Pitt, David C. 1972. *Using Historical Sources in Anthropology and Sociology.* New York: Holt, Rinehart and Winston.

Plattner, Stuart. 1974. Formal Models and Formalist Economic Anthropology: The Problem of Maximization. *Reviews in Anthropology* 1(4):572-81.

Powers, B., and G. Bultena. 1974. Correspondence between Anticipated and Actual Uses of Public Services by the Aged. *Social Service Review* 48:245-54.

Quinn, Naomi. 1978. Do Mfantse Fish Sellers Estimate Probabilities in Their Heads. *American Ethnologist* 5(2):206-26.

Radcliffe-Brown, A.R. 1940. On Social Structure. *Journal of the Royal Anthropological Institute* 70:1-22.

Rathbone-McCuan, E.E. 1981. A Step Toward Integrated Health and Mental Health Planning for the Rural Elderly. In *Toward Mental Health of the Rural Elderly*, edited by Paul K.H. Kim and Constance P. Wilson, 257-273, Washington, D.C.: Univ. Press of America.

Redfield, Robert. 1941. *The Folk Culture of the Yucatan.* Chicago: Univ. of Chicago Press.

Riley, M.W., M. Johnson and A. Foner. 1972. *Aging and Society*, vol. 3: *A Sociology of Age Stratification.* New York: Russell Sage Foundation.

Rose, A.M. 1964. A Current Theoretical Issue in Social Gerontology. *Gerontologist* 4(1):46-50.

———. 1965. The Subculture of the Aging: A Framework in Social Gerontology. In *Older People and Their Social World*, edited by A.M. Rose and W.A. Peterson, 3-16, Philadelphia: F.A. Davis.

Rosow, Irving. 1967. *Social Integration of the Aged.* New York: Free Press.

Ross, Jennie-Keith. 1977. *Old People, New Lives, Community Creation in a Retirement Residence.* Chicago: Univ. of Chicago Press.

Rowles, Graham D. 1978. *Prisoners of Space? Exploring the Geographical Experiences of Older People.* Boulder, Colo.: Westview Press.

Sahlins, Marshall. 1972. *Stone Age Economics*. Chicago: Aldine.

Salamon, Sonya. 1987. Ethnic Determinants of Farm Community Character. In *Farm Work and Fieldwork: American Agriculture in Anthropological Perspective*, edited by Michael Chibnick, 167-88. Ithaca, N.Y.: Cornell Univ. Press.

Salamon, Sonya, and Vicki Lockhart. 1980. Land Ownership and the Position of Elderly in Farm Families. *Human Organization* 39:324-31.

Sanday, Peggy Reeves. 1981. *Female Power and Male Dominance, On the Origin of Sexual Inequality*. New York: Cambridge Univ. Press.

Sanjek. Roger. 1978. A Network Method and its Use in Urban Ethnography. *Human Organization* 37(3):257-69.

SAS Institute. 1985. *SAS User's Guide: Basics Version*. 5th edition. Cary, N.C.: SAS Institute.

Schmitz-Scherzer, R. and U. Lehr. 1976. Interaction of Personality, SES, and Social Participation in Old Age. In *The Developing Individual in a Changing World*, vol. 2, edited by Klaus Riegel and John Meacham 621-27. Chicago: Aldine.

Schneider, David M. 1980. *American Kinship, A Cultural Account*. 2d edition. Chicago: Univ. of Chicago Press.

Schneider, David M. and George C. Homans. 1955. Kinship Terminology and the American Kinship System. *American Anthropologist* 57:1194-1208.

Schneider, M.J., M. Danforth and D.F. Voth. 1980. Senior Center Participation: A Two-stage Approach to Impact Evaluation. Paper presented at Rural Sociological Society, Washington, D.C.

Schultz, J. H. 1980. *The Economics of Aging*. Belmont, Calif.: Wadsworth.

Simmons, Leo W. 1945. *The Role of the Aged in Primitive Society*. New Haven: Yale Univ.

Simons, Ronald L. 1984. Specificity and Substitution in the Social Networks of the Elderly. *International Journal of Aging and Human Development* 18(2):121-39.

Sokolovsky, Jay. 1985. Network Methodologies in the Study of Aging. prepared for *New Methods for Old Age Research: Anthropological Alternatives*, edited by Christine L. Fry and Jennie Keith, South Hadley, Mass.:Bergin and Garvey.

Sokolovsky, Jay and C. Cohen. 1978. The Cultural Meaning of Personal Networks for the Inner City Elderly. *Urban Anthropology* 7(4):323-342.

Soldo, E. 1980. America's Elderly in the 1980s. *Population Bulletin* 35:15-18.

Spradley, James P. 1979. *The Ethnographic Interview*. New York: Holt, Rinehart and Winston.

Staniland, Martin. 1985. *What is Political Economy? A Study of Social Theory and Underdevelopment*. New Haven: Yale Univ. Press.

Steinhauer, M.B. 1981. Obstacles to the Mobilization and Provision of

Services to the Rural Elderly. *Educational Gerontology: An International Quarterly* 5:399-407.

Stephens, Mary Ann Parris and Murray D. Bernstein. 1984. Social Support and Well-being Among Residents of Planned Housing. *Gerontologist* 24(2):144-48.

Stephenson, John B. 1968. *Shiloh: A Mountain Community.* Lexington: Univ. of Kentucky Press.

Steward, Julian H. 1955. *Theory of Culture Change.* Urbana: Univ. of Illinois Press.

Storey, R. 1962. Who Attends a Senior Activity Center. *Gerontologist* 2:216-22.

Streib, Gordon F. 1968. Disengagement Theory in Sociocultural Perspective. *International Journal of Psychiatry* 6(1):69-76.

Stroller, E.P. 1983. Parental Caregiving by Adult Children. *Journal of Marriage and the Family* 45:851-58.

———. 1985a. Elder-Caregiver Relationships in Shared Households. *Research on Aging* 7:175-93.

———. 1985b. Exchange Patterns in the Informal Support Networks of the Elderly: The Impact of Reciprocity on Morale. *Journal of Marriage and the Family* 47:335-42.

Struyk, R.J. 1977. The Housing Situation of Elderly Americans. *Gerontologist* 17:130-39.

Taietz, P. 1976. Two Conceptual Models of the Senior Center. *Journal of Gerontology* 31:219-22.

Tesch, Stephanie, Susan Krauss Whitbourne and Milton F. Nehrke. 1981. Friendship, Social Interaction and Subjective Well-being of Older Men in an Institutional Setting. *International Journal of Aging and Human Development* 13(4):317-27.

Tyler, Steven A. 1969. *Cognitive Anthropology: Readings.* New York: Holt, Rinehart and Winston.

United States Bureau of the Census. 1932. *Fifteenth Census of the United States: 1930.* Agriculture, vol. 2, pt. 2. Washington, D.C.: U.S. Government Printing Office.

———. 1952. *United States Census of Agriculture: 1950,* vol. 1, *Counties and State Economic Areas,* pt. 19. Washington, D.C.: U.S. Government Printing Office.

———. 1961. *United States Census of Agriculture: 1959. vol. 1,* Counties. pt. 30, Kentucky. Washington, D.C.: U.S. Government Printing Office.

van Willigen, John and Billie R. DeWalt. 1985. *Training Manual in Policy Ethnography.* Special Publication of the American Anthropological Association, no. 19. Washington, DC: American Anthropological Association.

van Willigen, John, Thomas A. Arcury, and Robert G. Cromley. 1985.

Tobacco Men and Factory Hands: The Effects of Migration Turnaround and Decentralized Industrialization on the Social Lives of Older People in a Rural Kentucky County. *Human Organization* 44(1):50-57.

Vogt, Evon Z. 1960. On the Concepts of Structure and Process in Cultural Anthropology. *American Anthropologist* 62(1):18-33.

Wagner, Edwin E. 1960. Differences between Old and Young Executives on Objective Psychological Test Variables. *Journal of Gerontology* 15:296-99.

Walter, Adrian Ruth. 1985. The Mediating Role of Social Networks in the Housing Decisions of the Elderly. In *Social Bonds in Later Life*, edited by Warren A. Peterson and Jill Quadagno, 187-210. Beverly Hills, Calif.: Sage.

Walton, J. 1979. Urban Political Economy. *Comparative Urban Research* 7:9

Wardwell, John M. 1982. The Reverse of Nonmetropolitan Loss. In *Rural Society in the U.S.: Issues for the 1980s.*, edited by Don A. Dillman and Daryl J. Hobbs, 23-33. Boulder, Colo.: Westview Press.

Weicher, J.C. 1980. *Housing: Federal Policies and Programs*. Washington, D.C.: American Enterprise Institute for Rural Policy Research.

Wellman Barry and Alan Hall. 1986. Social Networks and Social Support: Implications for Later Life. In *Later Life, the Social Psychology of Aging*, edited by Victor W. Marshall, 191-231. Beverly Hills, Calif.: Sage.

Weiss, Lawrence and M.F. Lowenthal. 1975. Life Course Perspectives on Friendship. In *Four Stages of Life*, edited by M.F. Lowenthal, San Francisco: Jossey-Bass.

Wells, Miriam J. 1987. Sharecropping in the United States: A Political Economy Perspective. In *Farm Work and Fieldwork, American Agriculture in Anthropological Perspective*, edited by Michael Chibnik, Ithaca, N.Y.: Cornell Univ. Press.

Wentowski, Gloria J. 1981. Reciprocity and the Coping Strategies of Older People: Cultural Dimensions of Network Building. *Gerontologist* 21(6):600-09.

Wheeldon, P.D. 1969. The Operation of Voluntary Associations and Personal Networks in the Political Processes of an Inter-ethnic Community. In *Social Networks in Urban Situations*, edited by J. Clyde Mitchell, Manchester, Eng.: Manchester Univ.Press.

Wolfe, Alvin W. 1970. On Structural Comparisons of Networks. *Canadian Review of Sociology and Anthropology* 7(4):226-44.

Wylie, Mary. 1980. The Dying Community as a Human Habitat for the Elderly. In *The Dying Community*, edited by Art Gallaher, Jr. and Harland Padfield, 237-256. Albuquerque: Univ. of New Mexico Press.

Yearwood, Ann W. and Paula L. Dressel. 1983. Interracial Dynamics in a Southern Rural Senior Center. *Gerontologist* 23:512-17.

Youmans, E.G. 1967. *Older Rural Americans*. Lexington: Univ. of Kentucky Press.

Zborowski, M. and L.D. Eyde. 1962. Aging and Social Participation. *Journal of Gerontology* 17:424-30.

Zuiches, J.J. and D.L. Brown. 1978. The Changing Character of the Nonmetropolitan Population, 1950-1975. In *Rural U.S.A.: Persistence and Change*, edited by T.R. Ford, 55-72. Ames: Iowa State Univ. Press.

Index